The Harlot Church System

"Come out of her, My people"

The Harlot Church System
"Come out of her, My people"

Charles Elliott Newbold, Jr.

Ingathering Press

Published by Ingathering Press
P. O. Box 31795
Knoxville, TN 37930-1795
USA

Unless otherwise noted, scripture quotations are taken from the King James Version of the Bible with certain words changed to their modern equivalent; for example, "thee" and "thou" have been changed to "you," and "saith" has been changed to "says." Some words and punctuation marks have been modernized.

Scripture quotations noted NKJV are from The Holy Bible, New King James Version, Thomas Nelson Publishers. Copyright © 1983 by Thomas Nelson, Inc.

Scripture quotations noted NAS are from the New American Standard Bible. Copyright © 1960, 1963, 1968, 1971, 1973, 1975, 1977 by The Lockman Foundation.

Certain portions of scripture are italicized by the author to emphasize a point that is made about that scripture.

Some names of people and certain details have been changed to protect the identities of people referred to in this book.

Library of Congress Catalog Card Number: 99-96497

ISBN 0-9647766-3-4

Printed in the United States of America

Contents

Thanks to the many "brethren" who labored with me through the many edits of this book to assure, as best we can, that what is written herein is presented clearly and, more importantly, that it is spirit and truth. Though you will remain nameless, I want you to know how very much I appreciate you. You know who you are. Thanks for your input and encouragement.

Chapter 1

Zion and Babylon Compared

*W*e often sang scripture songs about Zion. I was a new convert then, gathering with a room full of very Spirit-sensitive believers. Those songs always struck a chord of joy in my heart, but I didn't know why. "Do you know what Zion is?" I asked one of the sisters.

"Yes." She meekly answered.

"Would you explain it to me?" I eagerly asked.

"You'll discover it in time."

"That's it!? You know the answer, but I'll have to wait to discover it myself?" Having no other choice, I waited.

Some years later I came to understand that *Zion is a symbolic place in the spirit where Jesus is the only thing there is*. He alone takes preeminence.

Then, I came to understand that Babylon meant something as well, that it stood in contrast to Zion. Symbolically, *Babylon is all that the carnal (fleshly) mind devises in the exaltation of Self—the preeminence of Self over God*. It is a place in us where we think we are *IT*. We exalt our imaginations and every high thing above the knowledge of God. 2 Cor. 10:5.

Both Zion and Babylon were historical places, yet the scriptures also speak of them as spiritual states of being. Hebrews 12:22 speaks of Zion (Sion, in KJV) in this figurative sense: "But we are come unto mount Sion, and unto the city of the living God, the heavenly Jerusalem, and to an innumerable company of angels, to the general assembly and assembly of the firstborn, which are written in heaven, and to God the Judge of all, and to the spirits of just men made perfect." 1 Peter 2:6 reads, "Behold, I lay in Sion a chief corner stone, elect, precious; and he who believes on Him shall not be confounded." This Zion is Jesus.

Revelation 14:8 is a good example of how Babylon has been used in this figurative sense: "And there followed another angel, saying, 'Babylon is fallen, is fallen, that great city, because she made all nations drink of the wine of the wrath of her fornication...'" Most notable is Revelation 17:5 which identifies the mother of harlots as Babylon: "Upon her forehead was a name written, "MYSTERY,

BABYLON THE GREAT, THE MOTHER OF HARLOTS, AND OF THE ABOMINATIONS OF THE EARTH."

Both Zion and Babylon mirror the condition of our hearts.

Symbolic Babylon is that attitude of the heart that makes us think we can solve all of our problems and meet all of our needs without God. We look to government, politics, science, technology, psychology, sociology, economics, entertainment, and religion for our help—things mankind has invented. Therefore, we look to ourselves to save ourselves.

In this book, however, my reference to spiritual Babylon is limited to the institutionalized, organized, religious *church* systems which I contend are products of the carnal mind. Please read on to see what I mean by this.

(The word *church* and the pronoun *it* when used in italics in this book refers to this Thing we call *church*. When it is not in italics, I am referring to buildings that have been dedicated to the worship of a deity, or I am directly quoting other sources.)

SPIRIT AND FLESH

In order to understand these two "spiritual states of being"— that is, Zion and Babylon—we must understand the difference between Spirit and flesh.

In the context of this book, the difference between the body of Christ and this Thing we call *church* is that difference between Spirit and flesh—what is of the Spirit of God and what is of our old man nature of flesh and sin, even the carnal mind.

Zion represents the Spirit; Babylon represents the flesh. The body of Christ needs very much to discern between what is Spirit and what is flesh, for that which is of the flesh is an enemy to the Spirit. True believers in Christ have been given the power of the Spirit to live a life separated from the flesh. This separation is what we call sanctification.

The word flesh is used in both the Old and the New Testament in reference to the natural, physical existence of all mankind such as we see it used in Matthew 24:22: "And unless those days were shortened, no *flesh* would be saved; but for the elect's sake those days will be shortened."

Flesh has also been used in reference to an individual's human body. After His resurrection and before His ascension, Jesus appeared to His followers and said, "Behold My hands and My feet, that it is I Myself. Handle Me and see, for a spirit does not have *flesh* and bones as you see I have." Luke 24:39.

However, the kind of flesh written about in this book is in reference to that fallen nature of sin within all mankind that came about when Adam rebelled in the garden. Paul wrote regarding this, "Now the works of the *flesh* are evident, which are: adultery, fornication, uncleanness, lewdness, idolatry, sorcery [which is witchcraft], hatred, contentions, jealousies, outbursts of wrath, selfish ambitions, dissensions, heresies, envy, murders, drunkenness, revelries, and the like; of which I tell you beforehand, just as I also told you in time past, that those who practice such things will not inherit the kingdom of God." Gal. 5:19-21. Flesh is capable of committing the most vile evils without conscience even while having an awareness of what is good and evil. Such occurred in the days of Noah. Gen. 6:5-7. These practices are not the deeds of the physical body, but of that fallen sin nature that resides in us.

Paul had already established in Galatians 5:17 that "the flesh lusts [sets its desire] against the Spirit, and the Spirit against the flesh; and these are contrary to one another, so that you do not do the things that you wish." Romans 8:7 attests that "the carnal mind is at enmity [hostile] against God; for it is not subject to the law of God, nor indeed can be."

The carnal mind and the Spirit of God speak languages that are foreign and unknown to each other. The carnal (fleshly) mind cannot speak Spirit and the Spirit of God cannot speak flesh. The carnal mind has no ability whatsoever to understand the things of God which are Spirit. 1 Cor. 2:12-14. When inspired things of God are reduced to rigid doctrines, systems of theology, reasoning and logic, they are no longer Spirit but have become flesh. And if flesh, then deception. The carnal mind is at total odds with the Spirit of God; it is hostile to God.

THE DEATH SENTENCE

The sentence of death has been pronounced over the flesh. The flesh nature of man is separated from God who is life; therefore, the flesh is dead and all that comes from the carnal mind is death.

Nevertheless, flesh has a life of its own. It is earthly, sensual, self-centered, and at war with God. Its life is born out of the seed of death. It has an inherent drive to preserve itself at all cost. It fears annihilation. Yet, it cannot save itself because it is destined to self-destruction. The flesh nature rules a person until the life of God in Christ is planted within his spirit, at which time the old seed of flesh and sin is understood to be what it already is—dead. Unfortunately, even after we are redeemed by the blood of the Lamb and while we remain in this life, we carry about both seeds: the seed of flesh and death, and the seed of Spirit and life.

THE HARLOT OF SELF

The flesh loves *Self*. Self with the capital "S" is the term I use throughout this book to refer to that the self-centered, self-indulging, self-absorbed, self-willed, self-serving nature of fallen flesh. The flesh nature of Self turns in on itself. It is selfish, prideful, arrogant, haughty, vain, narcissistic, manipulative, controlling, dominating, impatient, stubborn, insensitive, resentful, angry, unteachable, rebellious, fearful, anxious, complaining, disagreeable, judgmental, negative, critical, cynical, indifferent, greedy, lustful, sensual, envious, covetous, jealous, fault-finding, dishonest, and deceitful. It is deceived and suffers from delusions of grandeur. It always asks, "What's in it for me?"

The harlot, broadly defined, is anything for Self. I refer to these Things we call *church* as the harlot *church* system because they have been created out of our fleshly minds and desires for Self. *Churches* as we experience them today have no basis in scripture. They are icons of self-worship. Moreover, they are idolatrous, deceptive, and dangerous.

A TROUBLING MESSAGE

I will hit hard on the idolatry of the *church* system as we know it and experience it today. If you are not prepared to hear this message by the Spirit, you will no doubt take serious offense to it. The message of this book will be troubling to many of you who are victims of the *church* system, but will be most troubling to those of you who depend upon the *church* system for your livelihood and who find your significance, identity, validation, recognition, power, and security in *it*.

If you choose to continue reading this book, it will take you where you may think you do not want to go. You will journey beyond the facade of that Thing we call *church* and see how it is an invention of flesh. You will discover the demons that empower *it*. If you go the distance, you will hopefully find, with Abraham, that "city which has foundations, whose builder and maker is the Lord." Heb. 11:10. You will "come to Mount Zion, and to the city of the living God, the heavenly Jerusalem, and to an innumerable company of angels; to the general assembly and assembly of the firstborn, who are written in heaven, and to God the Judge of all, and to the spirit of just men made perfect." Heb. 12:22-23.

ZION AND BABYLON

Before I plunge forward into exposing the idolatry of this harlot system, I want to abbreviate some comparisons between spiritual

Zion, *where Jesus is the only thing there is,* and spiritual Babylon (the harlot), *where the carnal mind of Self exalts itself,* in order to provide a better point of reference for what follows. Many of the thoughts below are developed further throughout this book.

Zion refers to the true body of Christ, the bride, the ekklesia; Babylon refers to the false *church* system of men's traditions and religions. (Ekklesia is the Greek word in the New Testament which has been mis-translated "church" in most English versions, but it literally means "called-out-ones".)

Zion is a people—the people of God; Babylon is a Thing—*church* institutions and systems.

Zion is a living organism; Babylon is characterized by organizations, institutions, and systems.

Zion consists of people who have been born into it; Babylon consists of people who have joined it or been voted into it.

Zion is a people who are called by the name of Jesus; Babylon is a people who are called by many different names that represent divisions within this Babylonian *church* system: Baptist, Catholic, Charismatic, Episcopal, Lutheran, Methodist, Presbyterian, Pentecostal, and all the rest.

Zion is Jesus-centered; Babylon is self-centered.

Zion is living by the Spirit; Babylon is living after the flesh.

Zion is heavenly; Babylon is earthly.

Zion is grace; Babylon is law.

Zion is life; Babylon is death.

Zion is being; Babylon is doing.

Zion is rest; Babylon is works.

Zion is light; Babylon is darkness.

Zion is humility; Babylon is full of pride, arrogance, and haughtiness.

Zion is liberty in Christ; Babylon is bondage to the flesh.

Zion is the Kingdom of God; Babylon is the kingdoms of men.

Zion has Jesus Christ as her head; Babylon has elected or appointed men as their heads.

Zion is a Spirit-led people; Babylon is led by rules and regulations of man's own making.

Zion is Spirit-sensitive; Babylon is man-pleasing.

Zion is obedience to the Holy Spirit; Babylon is busy *church* work.

Zion accomplishes things in Holy Spirit power (Zech 4:6); Babylon tries to accomplish things in self-strength.

Zion has its authority in the Word of God; Babylon places its authority in man-made doctrines.

Zion is one body in Christ Jesus as Lord; Babylon is sectarian and divisive, consisting of many divisions of people.

Zion worships in spirit and in truth; Babylon programs praise.

Zion preaches Christ and Him crucified; Babylon proclaims denominations, doctrines, heritage, traditions, creeds, personal views and opinions.

Zion is the priesthood of all believers; Babylon is the clergy system. The clergy are those who want to make a difference between themselves and others.

Zion answers to God as the highest authority; Babylon answers to men and their institutions as the authority.

Zion calls forth revelation; Babylon depends upon imagination.

Zion conforms people into the image of Jesus; Babylon conforms people into its own image.

Zion decreases that Christ may increase; Babylon increases itself in power, position, riches, and domination.

Zion counts the cost; Babylon counts the money.

Zion lays down its life; Babylon preserves and protects itself.

Zion waits upon God to raise up what God wants in His timing; Babylon schemes, organizes, and promotes to execute its own plan in its own way and time.

Zion seeks the Lord with a whole heart to be possessed by Him; Babylon goes after things and people to possess them.

Zion is the city of God; Babylon seeks to build a city, a tower, and a name for itself. Gen. 11:4.

Zion longs to be gathered into Jesus; Babylon passionately seeks to gather people unto itself.

DENY SELF

To be a disciple of Jesus Christ one must be willing to deny Self, take up his cross, and follow Jesus. Luke 9:23. Self-denial is the cross we bear. The old man of flesh and sin has to be rendered dead. The laid-down life defines the New Testament concept of agape (love).

When we live according to the flesh, we are living for Self. Conversely, when we are living for Self, we are living according to the flesh. When we live according the Spirit, we will bear the fruit of agape. We have not been called to live unto ourselves. We have been called to surrender our lives to Christ that He might live His life of agape through us. We cannot be the bride of Christ and at the same time live selfishly in this world. We are either the bride or we are living the life of the harlot.

Self-centered living is making ourselves out to be god; therefore, it is idolatry. I will show in a subsequent chapter that idolatry is spiritual harlotry. I will also show how this Thing we call *church* is an idolatrous extension of ourselves—thus, spiritual harlotry.

We become spiritual prostitutes when we create something and give our hearts to it rather than to the Lord Jesus Christ. That is what men have done with this Thing we call *church*. They have made *church* a substitute for Jesus. Many within these harlot *church* systems are true believers who love the Lord, but are uninformed and deceived. They have unintentionally given their hearts to these Things we call *church*. God loves us all but hates our idolatries.

Judge the words in this book for yourself and judge yourself by these words. Open your heart to the Holy Spirit that He might instruct you and point you to Jesus. I hope to reveal Father-God's heart to you that your heart may be revealed to you; that you may dare face your idolatries, cleanse His temple of whom you and I are, and return to the God of your salvation. The idolatry revealed in this book is not about "them" but about each of us.

Chapter 2

Show the House to the House

*W*ith much fervor Brother Leonard, the visiting preacher, began his message by asking the congregation to turn to the gospel of John, chapter 15. He readily established that Jesus is the true vine and we were the branches. Then he made a startling point of saying that fruit-bearing was not the most important issue in this passage; abiding was. "Bearing fruit is mentioned four times," he pointed out, "while abiding is mentioned nine times." He hammered repeatedly the phrase, "We must abide." "We must abide." I waited for him to complete his sentence by saying, "We must abide in the vine who is Jesus." He never did. Then I saw it coming. He had to say it. It was the abundance of his heart. He was, after all, a *church* man. He stepped back from the podium, pointed an accusatory finger at his unsuspecting victims in the congregation, and said, "The problem we have in society today, and especially in the church, is people don't abide. They go from church to church and never make a commitment to the church or to the pastor."

Did he actually believe that abiding in that system we call *church* is what it means to abide in Jesus? Did he believe that committing to a *church* or the pastor is the same as committing to Jesus? His conclusion was an outrageous misrepresentation of scripture, spoken for the benefit of that local pastor whose *church* had a history of losing members. Rather than liberating the saints to have a deeper relationship with their Lord, he set a snare to enslave them even more to that Thing we call *church*.

He did not set out to deliberately deceive the people. In all truthfulness, he was deceived himself. We have all been deceived. Lied to. Beguiled. This deception has been passed through the generations of Christians since at least the third century A.D. Those who perpetuate this lie are equally victims of it. This deception is so deep and cruel that we have believed it as the truth. We minister death with this deception, thinking we are offering life.

Worse yet, people are unknowingly missing out on their glorious union with Christ because they have been given a false assurance of their salvation. This beguilement has puffed us up in self-importance. It has caused many believers to forsake their first love, Jesus. The devil has seduced us into dancing with him while making us think we were dancing with the Lord.

THE LIE

This is the lie: We have been made to believe that this Thing we call *church* is of God and that our membership and participation in it is essential to our Christian walk when in fact it is an idolatrous substitute for Jesus and quite often a hindrance to our walk with Him.

This Thing we call *church*, as we have come to experience *it*, is an idolatrous extension of our own Selves. Though it exists as an entity unto *it*self, we are in *it* and *it* is in us. *It* is an icon of self-worship that has grown out of the traditions of men and has no basis in scripture. We proclaim that this Thing we call *church* is the Kingdom of God when in fact it has nothing to do with the Kingdom of God. Rather, *it* is the modern-day Babylonian captivity of the elect of God.

We have confused our relationship with Christ by fusing it with this Thing we call *church*. We are led to believe that when we are in a proper relationship with *it* we are in a proper relationship with Christ; that we have to be a member of a *church* to be saved or to be a good Christian; that serving *it* is serving Christ; that loving *it* is loving Christ; that tithing to *it* is tithing to Christ.

In many instances this Thing we call *church* is like a tent we have made to spread over the moves and revelations of God in order to preserve them, touch them, contain them, maintain them, manipulate them, own and control other people in them, and use the people and the system for our sordid, fleshly gain. We find comfort in the restrictions these *church* walls set for us. We can hide in them and feel good in them. We widen these tent pegs just enough to let others in who want to walk, talk, and dress as we do.

We talk about this Thing we call *church* in strange ways. Where do you go to *church*? What is the name of your *church*? How was *church* today? Are you building an annex onto your *church*? Wow, did we ever have *church* at prayer meeting last night! The pastor or priest often greets the Sunday morning crowd, saying, "Good morning, *Church*." These statements make *church* out to be a building, an institution with a name, a service, a meeting, the kind of time we have together, and people.

The word "church" as it is used in English translations of the New Testament refers to the people of God, but we no longer limit its meaning to people. If we really meant that people are the "church" when we use that term, these same statements would have to be made this way: Where do *you* go to *you*? What is the name of *you*? How was *you* today? Are you building an annex onto *you*? Wow, did we ever have *us* at prayer meeting last night. We know better and insist in theory that we, the redeemed people of God, are the church. Yet, in practice, we make no distinction between the people and this Thing we call *church*. That the word church is used interchangeably this way is not the problem though. Much more is going on here than meets the eye.

The word *church*, as we use it, speaks of an illegal, unholy mystical union which embodies buildings, institutions, denominations, and people. These have been so fused and confused with each other that they perpetuate the dangerous lie that this Thing we call *church* (buildings, institutions, denominations, and the people associated with them) is Christ's assembly of called-out-ones. This Thing we call *church* looks good in its outward appearance, but is often inwardly controlled by men and women ambitiously, often unknowingly, seeking something for themselves.

SUBSTITUTE FOR JESUS

When we preach *church*, as we craftily do, we thereby preach another gospel, a false gospel. We perpetuate the lie. We are often zealous to evangelize people into our *churches*; yet, we are uncomfortable calling them to deny themselves and take up their crosses to follow Jesus. Such a command by Jesus is a foreign concept to most Christians today. If we happen to lead someone to Christ, we immediately impose *church* membership upon them, especially hoping that they will join "our" *church*.

I have personally longed to be in fellowship with other believers who were willing to *be* the body of Christ with me without having to sign on to the bondage and play the games that come with being a member of one of these institutions. I find no satisfaction in paying my dues to *church* just to "shake and howdy" with a few other believers while hiding behind our phony religious facades.

If it were true that going to *church* is synonymous with coming to Jesus, then we would have to ask: Which Jesus is it? Is it the Baptist Jesus? The Church of Christ Jesus? The Methodist Jesus? The Presbyterian Jesus? The Roman Catholic Jesus? The Orthodox Jesus? The Protestant Jesus? The Charismatic or Pentecostal Jesus? The Independent Jesus? There are so many to choose from. Unchurched people look at this mix of *churches* they are invited to join and wonder why anyone would want to be a part of that.

We give our hearts to these Things we call *church* rather than to the Lord Jesus Christ. They are enemies of God because they stand in place—in substitution—to what is holy, to what is His.

SHOW THE HOUSE TO THE HOUSE

This deception is not new. The children of Israel in Judah and Samaria were spiritually blinded by their own harlot hearts. They refused to hear the words of the prophets to return to the worship of their God. So, God scattered the people of Samaria to Assyria and later exiled Judah to Babylon.

The prophet Ezekiel had been carried away with the captives of Judah to Babylon. He had visions from God which he was told to tell the "stiff-faced" and "hard-hearted" elders of Judah whether they listened to him or not. God wanted them to know that a prophet had been in their midst. Ezek. 2-3.

Twenty-five years later, God took Ezekiel by way of a vision to the land of Israel and showed him a man whose appearance was like brass. This man had a line of flax and a measuring reed in his hand. He measured all around the Temple. He measured the width and the height of the wall, the gateways, chambers, and courts. Afterwards, he took Ezekiel to the gate that faced the east, and the glory of the God of Israel came from the east. "His voice was like the sound of many waters; and the earth shone with His glory." Ezek. 43:2. The Spirit lifted Ezekiel up and took him into the inner court as the glory of the Lord filled the Temple. Ezek. 43:5.

Then Ezekiel heard the Lord speaking to him from out of the house and told him that this house, the temple, was the place of His throne, the place of the soles of His feet, where He would dwell in the midst of the children of Israel forever. It would be the place where His holy name would dwell. Ezek. 43:7. God told Ezekiel that the house of Israel would not defile His house any more by their whoredoms; neither they, nor their kings, nor by the carcasses of their kings in their high places. Ezek. 43:6-9.

Then the Lord charged Ezekiel to show the condition of the house of the Lord to the house of Israel saying, "You son of man, *show the house to the house* of Israel, that they may be ashamed of their iniquities: and let them measure the pattern. And if they are ashamed of all that they have done, show them the form of the house, and the fashion thereof, and the going out thereof, and the coming in thereof, and all the forms...ordinances...and laws thereof...this is the law of the house: upon the top of the mountain the whole limit thereof round about shall be most holy." Ezek. 43:10-12.

Next, Ezekiel was shown a temple of stone. From the New Testament perspective we believe this temple of stone represents

God's spiritual house of lively stones—the body of Christ which is the temple of the Holy Spirit of whom we are. The condition of their hearts reflected the condition of God's temple. Conversely, the condition of God's temple reflected the condition of their hearts. It still works this way.

Centuries later, the aging apostle John was given the revelation of Jesus in which he was asked to measure the temple again. He wrote, "There was given me a reed like a rod: and the angel stood, saying, 'Rise, and measure the temple of God, and the altar, and those who worship therein.'" Rev. 11:1.

Today, the Spirit of the Lord calls out for us to *show the house to the house* that we might be ashamed of all that we have done; that is, show how we have given our hearts to our denominations, institutions, buildings, stained-glass windows, memorialized pews, patron saints, rituals, liturgies, doctrines, rules of order, programs, the Sunday morning service—so many, many things. The Spirit of the Lord wants to show us how we seek after our own agendas though they contradict the agenda of God. He calls us to keep His pattern, not ours; His laws, not ours. For this is the law of the house that we should be holy (separated) unto the Lord. Ezek. 43:12.

If we were asked to measure a physical house structure, we would pull out our measuring tape and calculate numbers. We would check the width, length, and height. Those who are in the institutional *church* typically measure themselves by how many members they have, how big their buildings are, how many buildings they have, how tall their steeple is, how many cars can be parked in their lot, what kind of cars are parked in their lot, how much money they take in. They measure these Things because they give the greater honor to those pastors and ministries who have the biggest and most. This is a false house.

The true house of God is measured by love, faith, mercy, grace, peace, life, light, rest, joy, hope, forgiveness, acceptance, righteousness, praise, worship, turning the other cheek, submitting to each other, receiving the prophet in the name of the prophet, employing the gifts of the Spirit for the building up of the body, having a passion for Jesus, and being excited about the things that excite God. These are expressions that define our relationship with Christ as His bride and with one another as the household of God. We measure the temple of the Holy Spirit of whom we are by these Biblical terms. If that which we are in that we call *church* is characterized by such terms as dissension, backbiting, dead works, unbelief, legalism, manipulation, and fear, then it is a harlot's house. We have a Thing—an idolatrous extension of Self that is not of God.

Chapter 3

Church: The Thing

*W*e were few in number as we sat comfortably face to face in the living room of a godly couple's house. I had something to share that Wednesday night. It was the first and most significant revelation that I had received from the Holy Spirit since my conversion a couple of years before.

I titled the teaching *The Thing*. A horror movie had been made years before by that same title. I assured my audience that I was not going to be talking about that. However, the Thing I talked about was just as monstrous. I began that teaching by saying, "That which we call the *church* is not the church but is a Thing." With that teaching, I began my personal journey in discovering the idolatry of the *church* and the difference between *it* and the true bride of Christ.

Years later, my wife and I were living in west Tennessee and were waiting for direction from the Lord. While there, He led me to start a meeting on Sunday mornings and invite some people I knew to come. Some of them came. We gathered in the name of Jesus. We sang; I shared the revelations and teachings the Lord gave me; we prayed, dismissed, and went our way. We were fairly close to one another and had some contact with each other during the week. We were beginning to *be* the body of Christ to one another.

Then, we bought a building, renovated it, opened the doors, and had our gatherings there. We called the building "The Christian Teaching Center." I did what I believed the Lord said to do and people began to come.

We were free of men's burdensome traditions, formalities, creeds, rules and regulations, and programs. We were committed to following the Holy Spirit wherever He chose to take us. His presence was powerfully felt in most of our gatherings in those early days.

I insisted that we were not a *church*, that God had not called me to start a *church*, and that I was not to be the pastor of a *church*. I tried to make a distinction between the building, which we had given a name, and those of us who gathered in that building, whom I refused to name. I explained that this was a teaching center for the body of Christ in that area. Perhaps it was a mistake, but we held Sunday morning meetings for those who chose not to go elsewhere. That Sunday morning meeting became the main event of the week.

The pressure was on. Some who came there wanted it to be a *church* and wanted me to be their pastor. I was pastoring individuals, but I insisted we were not a *church*.

A local pastor disputed my contentions, insisting that we were a *church*. He contended that there was no scriptural precedent for the para-*church* ministry that we had. He said, "If you look like a duck, walk like a duck, and quack like a duck, you must be a duck. You look like a *church*, walk like a *church*, and talk like a *church*." I did not want to hear that then, but looking back I had to admit he was right. This Thing we call *church* had weaseled its way into our work. The work at the Teaching Center was never supposed to be a *church*.

Once we began to "have" *church*, we began seeking something for ourselves. We created a Thing that had gone beyond what God had called me to do. We went back to the very thing that we had come out of. We had Sunday morning and Sunday evening services, Sunday School, and a youth program. We took up offerings and put them in a bank account. Our group became known by the name I had put on the building.

I lost my vision to build up a people and began, instead, to build up a Thing. We began to go after *it* instead of going after the Lord Jesus Christ. We gathered around *it* instead of the presence of the Lord. People started leaving and they did not know why. The more they left, the more I tried to hold on to them. I felt abandoned. But it was I who had abandoned them by allowing the work to become a Thing. Not long after that, Ichabod was written over our door, spiritually speaking. 1 Sam. 4:21. As with Elijah, the brook dried up and the ravens ceased to bring their morsels. 1 Kings 17:3-7. It was time for us to move on. It took a year for me to muster enough courage to finally shut *it* down.

While most of us know that the word "church" as it is used in scripture refers to the people of God in Christ, we nevertheless have made a Thing of *it*. It is an extension of ourselves and exists as an entity unto itself.

THE EVOLUTION OF *CHURCH*

How did this Thing we call *church* evolve?

Believers in the New Testament did not have such baggage. At first they were simply called the followers of the way. They gathered spontaneously in the temple and in some synagogues for a period of time. Mostly, however, they met in private homes and went from house to house. They were drawn together by the presence of the Lord in their midst.

Christians did not have church buildings until Constantine the Great, Emperor of Rome from 306 to 337 A.D., embraced Christianity. His endorsement of the faith created a free climate for men to erect buildings "to the glory of their God."

The earliest church buildings are believed to have been built after the pattern of the Roman basilica—architecture that was firmly rooted in the traditions of the Roman empire and has no basis in scripture. Church buildings became more elaborate with the Byzantine, Romanesque, and Gothic influences. The layout of these cathedrals often hid the monks and choirs from the people, advancing the idea of the separation of clergy from laity which is unfounded in scripture.

During the reformation, Protestants halted the building of great edifices. The reformers were content with simple, rectangular buildings. They were primarily interested in gathering the people and having a place to preach. By the nineteenth century, however, Protestant church architecture had likewise become elaborate and consisted of elements from a variety of styles.

The enchantment with church buildings throughout the centuries has contributed to the institutionalization of the *church* system as we now know it.

THE ETYMOLOGY OF THE WORD "CHURCH"

With the inclination toward the construction of buildings for the worship of God, it is little wonder that the translators of the King James Version of the Bible chose to translate the Greek word *ekklesia* by using the English word "church." A deeper look at the etymology of the word "church" is quite revealing.

Moving backwards into time, the word "church" was derived from the Old English word *cirice* which is related to the Norwegian/Scandinavian word *kirkja*. These were derived from the Germanic word *kirka*; which was derived from the late Greek word *Kyrite*; which was derived from the Greek word *kurios* which means "ruler," "lord," "master." In the Greek, *Kuriake oika* means "lord's house." Thus, the word church came to mean "a building set apart or consecrated for public worship."[1]

Though the word "church" does not have its root in the Greek term *ekklesia*; it is used to translate *ekklesia*. *Ekklesia* is the for-

---

[1] *Webster's New World Dictionary*, 2nd college ed., s.v. "church."

mation of two Greek words: *ek* which means "out of" and *kaleo* which means "to call." Combined, the word literally means "to call out of." *Ekklesia* was commonly used among the Greeks in reference to a body of citizens who "gathered" to discuss the affairs of state.[2] A correct and quite appropriate translation of *ekklesia* is "called-out-ones" although there are times when the context demands that "assembly" or "gathering-of-called-out-ones" be used. The word has to do with a people who are called-out to be gathered together.

Perhaps the translators of the King James version of the Bible had in mind that the body of Christ could be thought of as a spiritual *kuriake oika* (Lord's house) since we are the temple of the Holy Spirit. 1 Cor. 3:16. Perhaps. But, from that time to this, the word *church* is used to refer to more than people. Its use has been so adulterated that we ought never to use it when we are referring to the body of Christ. It is appropriate to use the word "church" when we are actually talking about a building but not when we are talking about the body of Christ. What we call *church* is a Thing. The ekklesia is a people.

THE THING

We organize this Thing. We name *it*, incorporate *it*, elect officers to *it*, open bank accounts in *its* name, and train and hire staff to run *it*. We take up money for *it*. We devise campaigns to recruit more people to join *it*. We track attendance to *it*. We love *it*, get mad at *it*, resign from *it*, and leave *it*. If we are particularly fond of *it*, we make up brochures and buy ads to market *it*.

We evaluate the Thing to determine *its* success or failure. "The praise service was good," we might say. "The sermon was okay." "The offering was poor." "The attendance was down."

Ask a pastor how his *church* is coming along and he may answer with such comments as: "Oh, our building program is great." "We're getting in members left and right." "We've doubled our membership in the last year." "We are losing people out of the back door as fast as they come in the front." See where his heart is? He is evaluating the *thing* over which he is likely the head. The growth of his *church* reflects upon his success or failure as its leader. If, on the other hand, he answers regarding the spiritual well-being of the people, he understands more of what it means to be the body of Christ. "Well, you know, many of them have endured some afflic-

---

[2] *Vine's Complete Expository Dictionary of Old and New Testament Words*, N.T., s.v. "assembly."

tion, but it has made them stronger in the Lord."

If he talks about *his* people in a possessive sense, he is snared by his own conceit. They are not *his* people. On the other hand, if he talks about the sheep who belong to the good shepherd who is Jesus Christ, he may be free and more likely to set God's people free.

FOR THE SAKE OF IT

Soon after a *church* is started, *it* nearly always takes on an existence of *its* own and begins to exist for *its* own sake. The people in *it* exist to serve *it* rather than *it* existing to serve the people. Those dedicated to keeping the *church* going expect their members to attend *it*, support *it*, and serve *it*. They plan various programs that fit the model of what they think a full service *church* ought to look like.

The Conners family had been supported by their *church* for eight years of difficult but faithful duty on the mission field. After their return, they attended their *church* for awhile before dropping out. The first pastoral or administrative inquiry about them was by the *church* accountant. "Are the Conners attending church?" "No," a friend of theirs answered. "Why?" "For no particular reason." He was indignant. "After all the money we've given them, now when they could help they're not around." Perhaps that would have been a genuine concern under other circumstances, but his interest in them came one and a half years after their return. As Mrs. Conners regretfully said, "I was frustrated by the obvious fact that no one on staff seemed to notice we were no longer going there and when they did notice, the first comment was about money." Had the money been spent on the Conners? No. They were in another land to be spent by the Lord for the sake of serving the saints there. It seems the Conners were expected to serve the institution, but were themselves abandoned by the so-called leadership within that institution.

Brother Billy became the pastor of West Side Church after his father died. His father founded the *church*. Brother Billy announced one Sunday that he was fulfilling his vision to have a jail and bus ministry. "We lack these things to be a complete *church*," he explained. "We need volunteers for the jail ministry and for the bus ministry. Sign-up sheets are on the back table." Many dear hearts who felt no calling for such service signed on to make Brother Billy feel okay about himself and his *church*. They had to serve him so he could fulfill his vision for a Thing.

People often grow weary of these works of men and drop out.

Leadership is hard to find. If the services or programs were really meeting people's needs, people would be more likely to support them. A lack of support may be a clear indication that the event no longer meets a need worth supporting.

PROVOKING GUILT

If we do not provide the expected support for the Thing and its programs, whether we want to or not, whether we are called to serve in a certain capacity or not, we are made to feel guilty. Have you ever felt guilty for missing a function of the *church?* Those little shame-based voices in your head whisper "naughty, naughty." "It was my fault the program failed. I didn't give enough of my time and money to *it.*" You can know by those feelings of guilt that you are serving a Thing and not the Master.

When we are asked by leadership in the *church* to make a commitment to the *church,* we are actually being asked to make a commitment to the Thing. Our loyalty is measured by how well we serve this Thing. We are thought to be slothful Christians if we do not support *it;* and if we do not even attend a local *church,* we are assumed to be backsliders.

On the other hand, when we "do" *church,* we have expectations that *it* ought to be a certain way. *It* has to work according to our expectations, or we will feel like *it* has failed.

If the Thing has to work a certain way before *it* is successful, then those who support *it* will be pressured into performing in such a way as to make *it* a success. If *it* is not a success, someone is to blame. It is either the people's fault, the pastor's fault, the choir director's fault, or the *church* board's fault.

What if you and I have different expectations about how a *church* should work? We will have conflict. There will always be conflict in the *church* because there will always be expectations in conflict. These are man's expectations, not God's.

ADDICTED TO THE THING

Some people are clinically classified as religious addicts. I am a recovering *church*-addict. Soon after my conversion in 1978, I saw how this *church* Thing was an idolatrous system of men's traditions. I despised *it* (not the people in *it);* yet, I felt a seductive pull back into *it.*

I needed *it.* I had previously found my identity in *it.* I had presence, power, and position in *it.* As the pastor of *it,* I thought I owned at least a part of *it.* My heart would secretly boast, "This is mine!" *It* was my source of financial support. *It* was the only thing I was trained to do. I was joined to *it* and *it* was joined to me.

We bond with that Thing we call *church* and thereby get in bondage to *it*. We join *it* and *it* somehow takes possession of us. We do, in fact, get addicted to *it*. As Dennis Loewen wrote, "It is addictive. How do we know? One way is that we all go through withdrawal when we leave it."

Some discerning believers who attend spiritually stagnant *churches* realize they no longer need to be there. The Holy Spirit is absent. The services are dead. The preacher is boring. People argue over petty, irrelevant issues. They feel their tithes are wasted on worthless salaries, programs, and mortgages. Their huge buildings stand empty more often than not. They feel obligated to serve on committees that serve the institution more than they serve the people. They see the leadership trying one gimmick after another to make the Thing relevant in order to get more people to join *it* and be active in *it*.

These precious believers want to leave but find that they cannot. Mother wouldn't understand. "Why, that stained glass window was dedicated in grandpa's name. How can you even think about leaving?" They rationalize that they have life-long friends there. "How can I leave them?" They are made to feel like traitors, deserters, troublemakers, or mavericks. Some people disown their own family members who leave their "faith." Some traditions believe that a person will go to hell if they leave their particular brand of *church*.

So, they feel stuck in the system. They put on their Sunday morning smiles and hide their secret resentments for feeling stuck. They shake and howdy down the aisle, pretending, "Isn't it good to be in the house of the Lord?" They settle into their familiar pews and begin again to fellowship with the backs of people's heads.

Many who dare to leave one *church* go down the street hoping for a better "spiritual climate" only to find the same old whore in a brand new dress. Only the rules are slightly different. They go from *church* to *church* looking for that which is genuine only to find more phony religious facades; they go looking for Spirit and truth only to find more flesh and hypocrisy. Yet, they continue their search, because they are addicted to *it*. They bob up and down on their wooden horses unable to dismount because of the velocity of that carousel—the *church* system that perpetually spins round and round, going nowhere.

A few discerning persons are able to break away from the bondage of *church*, but often leave damaged and resentful. Some of these attend anonymous groups, seeking recovery from the religious abuses inflicted upon them by these religious systems of men's traditions.

Church, as we have come to experience *it*, permeates every aspect of our society. *It* is the only thing we have seen and known that supposedly represents Christ. In going after *it*, just as did Israel of old, we have played the harlot and provoked the Lord to jealousy.

I hope you are praying for the Holy Spirit to lift the veil from over your eyes to see how *church* is a counterfeit system, to see how we have made a Thing out of who we are in Christ and gone after *it* instead of Jesus.

Chapter 4

Jealousy: Playing the Harlot

$\mathcal{M}$ost everyone in the small, rural *church* I was serving accepted the fact that I believed that speaking in tongues, divine healing, casting out demons, and all the gifts of the Holy Spirit were for today, even though the officialdom of that denomination disagreed. Nevertheless, I tried to make Jesus the only issue that mattered. Everyone was happy with that arrangement until the Holy Spirit spoke to my spirit requiring that I abolish the Sunday School.

"You're messing with my mind, Lord," I argued. "One doesn't abolish Sunday School, especially as a pastor in this denomination. The Sunday School belongs to the elders. You should know that, Lord." I dismissed the thought as reckless. I had plans to build up the Sunday School. Studies have shown that the existence of small groups such as the Sunday School class contribute to *church* growth, and at that stage in my understanding, I wanted to build up the *church*.

However, after being sternly directed to abolish the Sunday School for the third time, I knew I had to do something. I called the men of the *church* together and presented my dilemma to them. Most of them were willing to test it out to see what God might do. "After all," many of them reasoned with me, "if it doesn't prove profitable, we can always go back to having Sunday School."

Not every one was willing to test it out, however. I did not know why God wanted me to take such action until I tried to negotiate the deal with the main person of influence in the *church*. Tears welled up in her eyes as she spoke with a broken, yet, certain voice, "You're not going to take MY Sunday School away from me." Then I knew what this was about. Sunday School was a golden calf to some of them and I had dared to touch it.

IDOLATRY: THE EXTENSION OF SELF

Judson Cornwall aptly says, "Idolatry is principally the response of personal adoration toward something less than Jehovah God, whether that something is Self, an object made by ourselves, or a concept we may have embraced...An idol is anything or anyone, including ourselves, that is given the credit for the abilities that only God possesses."[3] Monty Stratton adds, "Any image we have of ourselves that is not God's image of us is an idol, a false God."[4]

We, as created human beings, make things and accomplish things that we come to adore. We set these things before us and pay homage to them whether they are the songs or novels we write, the athletes we create, the gardens we plant, the businesses we build, the trophies we win, the children we sire, the rockets we orbit, the cures we invent, the sermons we preach, or the *churches* we institute. We live vicariously through the idols we have made of movie stars, music stars, and sports stars. We want the power that we imagine fame and fortune would bestow upon us. We want to be god, especially over our own lives.

Though we are greater than the images we make, we still bow down and pay obeisance to them. We take such pride in our works. We allow them to control our lives, our emotions, and our relationships. We love them. We look at them, and our hearts swell with pride. They are idolatrous extensions of ourselves.

IDOLATRY: THE WORSHIP OF SELF

All idolatry is the worship of Self. It is an extension of ourselves: our adored opinions, speculations, plans, programs, and projects; it is the self-exalted work of our hands and the imaginations of our minds—all the things we do in our old man nature of flesh and sin that causes us to esteem ourselves more highly than we ought to. It is the attitude of the wicked stepmother in the story of Snow White who asks, "Magic mirror on the wall, who's the fairest one of all?" fully expecting for the mirror to answer, "You are the fairest one of all."

Idolatrous, fallen man is self-centered by nature. To be any different, we have to be transformed into a new creature. We need a new nature that gives us the desire to surrender Self for a higher good, namely, the life of Christ in us. Only Christ through His Spirit can implant that new nature within us.

Whatever appeals to Self is not of God. Self is in love with Self. It seeks its own. It is vain, prideful, arrogant, self-exalting, self-indulging, self-absorbed, power-hungry, and lustful. It strives for independence, self-reliance, and self-management. It uses and abuses others, if necessary, to achieve its own ambitions. It lies, steals, cheats, murders, covets, blames, justifies, and does whatever seems necessary to save itself. It goes to any end to protect it-

---

[3]Judson Cornwall, *Things We Adore: How to Recognize and Get Free of Idolatry* (Shippensburg, PA.: Destiny Image Publishers, 1991), 18.

[4]Monty Stratton, *The Unveiling* (Macon, GA: Foundation Ministries, 1998), 78.

self. It is addicted to more. It can never be satisfied.

The flesh nature of Self generally looks to its own inventions—science, government, military, religion, education, sports, and other human institutions and inventions—to save us, feed us, protect us, make us happy, give us our identity, and provide us with a better lifestyle. We create institutions to serve us, and we get angry when they fail us.

Because Self is centered upon itself, it is a black hole upon the space where it stands, forever suctioning itself inward as a vacuum. Self consumes itself, is self-destructive, and has death as its final reward. Self lives and dies for Self.

IDOLATRY: SELF-STRENGTH

The idolatry of Self is seen in our drivenness to accomplish things in our own strength. We see things to do, and we must do them. We are constantly distracted by the busyness we create for ourselves. Busyness is a distraction from intimacy with God. We would rather be *doing* something for God than spending time with Him. Yet, He did not create us to *do* for Him, but to *be* as He is that we might have fellowship with Him and with one another in Him.

We enslave ourselves to the works we require of ourselves. Moreover, we enslave others to our works when others allow us to do so. We adore our accomplishments. Consequently, we have even made idols out of our quiet time, Bible study, intercessory prayer, street witnessing, and other works that seem "good" to us. These are not wrong. They are wonderful when they are inspired by the Holy Spirit. They become idolatrous to us when we use them to make ourselves feel like we have done something for God.

IDOLATRY: THINGS THAT POSSESS US

Our idols have to do with those things that possess our hearts. Whatever we own, owns a part of us. In the Old Testament, Jacob served his father-in-law, Laban, for twenty years to earn his wives, Leah and Rachel, and to earn his flock so he could return to the land of his father. Because Laban restrained him from going, Jacob left Laban by stealth with his wives and animals. As she went out, Rachel stole her father's household idols to take with her. Gen. 31. These idols may have been valuable heirlooms and that could have played a part in her motives to carry them away, but more likely it was because her heart had already been carried away by them.

The things we go after usually overtake us. I lived in Nashville, Tennessee, the country music capital of the world, where there is a saying about many of those musical hopefuls who live there that they are "chasing the beast." This beast is an imaginary quest for significance through the fame many of them hope "making it in music" will bring them. It appears to me, though, that the beast is chasing them. The beast can be any of those things we seek for Self to possess. These things we seek often possess us. We can be possessed by quest.

A JEALOUS GOD

God created us for Himself. He wants intimate relationship with us. He wants us to know Him, love Him, trust Him, depend upon Him, and obey Him. He is a loving and faithful Father to us who believe and requires of us that we return love and faithfulness to Him. He is profoundly jealous of anything we put between Him and us. Allow yourself to feel God's passionate disdain for our idolatry as you carefully read the text below. You who truly love the Lord should be impacted forever by the quotes from scripture.

God spoke through Moses to the children of Israel, saying: "I am the LORD your God, who brought you out of the land of Egypt, out of the house of bondage. You shall have no other gods before Me. You shall not make unto you any graven image, or any likeness of anything that is in heaven above, or that is in the earth beneath, or that is in the water under the earth." You shall not bow down yourself to them, nor serve them..." Exod. 20:1-5; Deut. 5:1-10.

Jesus answered the Pharisee saying, "You shall love the Lord your God with all your heart, and with all your soul, and with all your mind. This is the first and great commandment." Matt. 22:37. This kind of love is agape, which has to do with surrendering your life for the well-being of others. In this case, it has to do with wanting only what God wants, wanting nothing for Self.

Idolatry breaks the heart of God who jealously wants our undivided love, worship, and faithfulness. God is jealous of our idols. He is jealous when we glory in ourselves and our achievements rather than recognizing that "every good gift and every perfect gift is from above, and comes down from the Father of lights." James 1:17. God said, "You shall not bow down yourself to them [other gods], nor serve them: for I the LORD your God am a jealous God." Exod. 20:1-5. His name is Jealous. Exod. 34:14.

Moses charged the people to keep God's ordinances and warned them not to commit idolatry saying, "The LORD your God is a consuming fire, even a jealous God." Deut. 4:24. Joshua reaffirmed to the people that God "is a holy God. He is a jealous God." Josh. 24:19.

Elijah expressed jealousy on God's behalf: "I have been very jealous for the LORD God of hosts: because the children of Israel have forsaken Your covenant, thrown down Your altars, and slain Your prophets with the sword; and I, even I only, am left; and they seek my life, to take it away." 1 Kings 19:14. [Also read: Ezek. 8:3; 16:38-42; 23:25; 36:5-6; 38:19; 39:25.]

Asaph lamented: "How long, LORD? Will You be angry forever? Shall Your jealousy burn like fire?" Ps. 79:5.

The prophet, Nahum, feeling the pulse of God, declared that "God is jealous, and the LORD revenges and is furious; the LORD will take vengeance on his adversaries, and He reserves wrath for his enemies." Nah. 1:2.

Joel, looking to a day of renewal, prophesied, "Then will the LORD be jealous for his land, and pity His people." Joel 2:18.

Zephaniah spoke, "Neither their silver nor their gold shall be able to deliver them in the day of the LORD's wrath; but the whole land shall be devoured by the fire of His jealousy: for He shall make even a speedy riddance of all them who dwell in the land." Zeph. 1:18. He continued to speak for God saying, "Therefore wait upon Me, says the LORD, until the day that I rise up to the prey: for My determination is to gather the nations, that I may assemble the kingdoms, to pour upon them My indignation, even all My fierce anger: for all the earth shall be devoured with the fire of My jealousy." Zeph. 3:8.

Zechariah wrote, "The angel that communed with me said unto me, You cry, saying, Thus says the LORD of hosts; I am jealous for Jerusalem and for Zion with a great jealousy." Zech. 1:14. And again, he wrote, "Thus says the LORD of hosts; I was jealous for Zion with great jealousy, and I was jealous for her with great fury." Zech. 8:2.

The apostle Paul asked the Corinthians, "Do we provoke the Lord to jealousy?" 1 Cor. 10:22. As did Elijah, Paul felt the fire of God's jealousy in his belly and wrote again later, "For I am jealous over you with godly jealousy: for I have espoused you to one husband, that I may present you as a chaste virgin to Christ." 2 Cor. 11:2.

ISRAEL: CHOSEN FOR A PURPOSE

Israel was chosen by God that He might have a people who were called by His name. Deut. 28:10; 2 Chron. 7:14; Dan. 9:19; Acts 15:14. They were to be a people through whom God would make a name for Himself. 2 Sam. 7:23; 1 Chron. 17:21. They would be to Him a people, a name, a praise, and a glory. Jer. 13:11.

Israel was to be a holy (separated) nation of people unto the Lord. It was three months after they left Egypt and were encamped in the Wilderness of Sinai that Moses went up on the mountain to talk to God. God told Moses to tell the people "You have seen what I did to the Egyptians, and how I bore you on eagles' wings, and brought you unto Myself. Now, therefore, if you will obey My voice indeed, and keep My covenant, then you shall be a peculiar treasure unto Me above all peoples: for all the earth is Mine: And you shall be unto Me a kingdom of priests, and a holy nation." Exod. 19:4-6.

The followers of Christ, whether Jew or Gentile, are the fulfillment of divine expectation. Peter wrote regarding those who believe in Jesus Christ, "But you are a chosen generation, a royal priesthood, a holy nation, a peculiar people; that you should show forth the praises of Him who has called you out of darkness into His marvelous light." 1 Pet. 2:9.

The Lord was to be their God and they were to be His people. They were not to have other gods before them. They were not to call upon the name of any other god and give that god the glory for the things that God had done for them. That would have been a great insult to God, to His name, and to those who were called by His name. God is zealously jealous of those things in which we put more confidence, comfort, and pleasure than in Him.

THE BAN

God knew that the only way to ensure that the Israelites would remain faithful to Him was to ban them from mingling with the heathens of the land. He made a covenant with them while they were in the wilderness. He told them that He would do marvels among them by driving out the Amorite, the Canaanite, the Hittite, the Perizzite, the Hivite, and the Jebusite from before them when they entered Canaan.

God warned them, however, to be careful not to make a covenant with the inhabitants of the land where they were going. Failure to destroy the idolatrous altars of the heathens, to break their images, and cut down their groves (places of idol worship) would be a snare in the midst of them. The Israelites would "take their daughters unto their sons, and their daughters [would] go a whoring after their gods, and make their sons go a whoring after their gods." Exod. 34:10-17.

The worship of other gods is idolatry, and idolatry is playing the harlot so far as God is concerned. God also calls it fornication and adultery. The King James version of the Bible translates it "a whoring." This radical language portrays the heart of God in the matter of idolatry. It should cause us to fall on our faces, quickly repent of our idolatries, and turn to Him with a pure, unadulterated heart.

THE VIOLATION OF GOD'S BAN

God told Israel not to mingle with the inhabitants of the land and go after their gods, but they did it anyway. God knew that they would do it. He told Moses that after he died "this people will rise up, and go a whoring after the gods of the strangers of the land where they are going and will forsake Me, and break My covenant which I had made with them. Then My anger shall be kindled against them in that day, and I will forsake them, and I will hide My face from them, and they shall be devoured, and many evils and troubles shall befall them; so that they will say in that day, Are not these evils come upon us, because our God is not among us? And I will surely hide My face in that day for all the evils which they shall have brought, in that they are turned unto other gods." Deut. 31:16-18.

Israel's failure in the wilderness

The Israelites violated God's ban while they were still in the wilderness. They were in a place called Shittim when they committed whoredom with the daughters of Moab. The Moabites seduced the Israelites to make sacrifices and bow down to their gods. Israel joined itself to Baal-peor, the idol god of Moab, and the anger of the LORD was kindled against Israel.

The LORD instructed Moses to take all the heads of those who had broken the ban, "and hang them up before the LORD against the sun, that the fierce anger of the LORD may be turned away from Israel." Moses, in turn, commanded the judges of Israel to kill their men who were bowing down to Baal-peor.

One of the Israelites shamelessly brought a Midianite woman to his brothers in full view of Moses and the people. Phinehas, the son of Eleazar, the son of Aaron the priest, saw it, rose up from among the people, and took a javelin in his hand. He went after the man of Israel into the tent and thrust both of them through. This brought an end to the plague upon the children of Israel that day. His jealousy for God turned away God's wrath. Twenty-four thousand people died in that plague. Num. 25:1-11.

Deuteronomy 32:16-17, and 21 tells us that the Israelites provoked God to jealousy with strange gods, and that these were abominations to Him. "They sacrificed unto devils, not to God; to gods whom they knew not"...to new gods whom their fathers had not even feared. "They have moved Me to jealousy," God said, "with that which is not God; they have provoked Me to anger with their vanities: and I will move them to jealousy with those who are not a people; I will provoke them to anger with a foolish nation."

27

Israel's failure during the judges

God brought Israel out of Egypt with attesting signs and wonders. They miraculously crossed through the Red Sea on dry ground. They were given the manna, water, and quail. They heard God on the mountain and saw His glory on Moses' face. They wandered for forty years, and their sandals did not wear out. They experienced the jealousy of God at Shittim. They entered the land of God's promise under the leadership of Joshua, miraculously crossing the Jordan river and taking Jericho with marching, the blowing of horns, and shouting.

They were supposed to drive out all of the inhabitants of the land lest they mingle with them and bow down to their gods. Many of the tribes of Israel did not do that. They did not utterly drive out the inhabitants of the land and were, thereby, disobedient to God.

An angel of the Lord came up from Gilgal to Bochim, and told the people of Israel, "I made you to go up out of Egypt, and have brought you unto the land which I swore unto your fathers; and I said, I will never break My covenant with you. And you shall make no league with the inhabitants of this land; you shall throw down their altars, but you have not obeyed My voice. Why have you done this? Wherefore I also said, I will not drive them out from before you, but they shall be as thorns in your sides and their gods shall be a snare unto you." The people lifted up their voice and wept at the words of the angel. Judg. 2:1-4.

Nevertheless, a new generation grew up after Joshua, and they also did the very thing that was evil in the sight of the Lord: they abandoned the Lord and served the idolatrous god and goddess, Baal and Ashtoreth. Judg. 2:13.

And so it happened, over and over again. God raised up individuals like Ehud, Deborah, Gideon, Samson, and other judges in Israel. The Israelites would not listen to their judges but went "a whoring" after other gods. After they fell under the oppressive hand of their enemies in the land, they repented and cried out to God, and He changed His mind and delivered them. (Read Judges 2:17-20.)

The period of the judges ended with this tragic commentary: "In those days there was no king in Israel: every man did that which was right in his own eyes." Judg. 21:25. Anarchy is the ultimate idolatry of Self.

Israel's failure during the kings

The Israelites wanted their own king like all of the other nations, thus rejecting God from reigning over them. So, God told Samuel to give them what they were asking for. 1 Sam. 8:5-7. How frightening that God might really give us what we think we need and want!

Nothing changed. They had harlot hearts. 1 Chronicles 5:25 reports that "they transgressed against the God of their fathers, and went a whoring after the gods of the people of the land, whom God destroyed before them."

The Psalmist laments: "They did not destroy the nations, concerning whom the LORD commanded them: But were mingled among the heathen, and learned their works. And they served their idols: which were a snare unto them. Yes, they sacrificed their sons and their daughters unto devils, and shed innocent blood, even the blood of their sons and of their daughters, whom they sacrificed unto the idols of Canaan: and the land was polluted with blood. Thus, they were defiled with their own works, and went a whoring with their own inventions." Ps. 106:34-39. This entire Psalm is a powerful recantation of Israel's forgetfulness.

GODS OF THE FLESH

The Israelites set up their own high places and made altars to Baal. They carved out Ashtoreths and bowed down to them. They sacrificed their children to Molech by making them walk through fire.

The chronicler of 1 Kings 14:22-23 wrote, "And Judah did evil in the sight of the LORD, and they provoked Him to jealousy with their sins which they had committed, above all that their fathers had done. For they also built them high places, and images, and groves, on every high hill, and under every green tree."

Asaph, the Psalmist, lamented the sins of the people against a jealous God singing, "For they provoked him to anger with their high places, and moved him to jealousy with their graven images." Ps. 78:58.

Baal means "master" or "lord" and has also been translated "husband." Baal was the farm god believed to be responsible for the increase of flocks, crops, and families.

"The worship of Baal, as it existed when Israel began to filter into Canaan, was conducted by priests in fields and on mountain 'high places' where communities brought 'taxes' to their favorite deity, in the form of wine, oil, first fruits, and firstlings of flocks. The cult included joyous, licentious dances and ritualistic meals."[5]

The *Ashtoreth* was the name given to the goddess of the moon, sexuality, sensual love, and fertility. It was also the name for the

---

[5] *Harper's Bible Dictionary* (New York: Harper & Brothers, 1956), s.v. "Baal."

wooden female figures or poles that were set up to represent her.[6] Her temples were centers of sacred prostitution. *Ashtoreth* is mentioned some forty times in the Old Testament.

Molech means "king." His worship was characterized by parents who sacrificed their children, compelling them to walk through or into a furnace of fire. Hebrew law strictly forbade this practice. The Lord had spoken to Moses saying, "Again, you shall say to the children of Israel, Whosoever of the children of Israel, or of the strangers that sojourn in Israel, who gives any of his seed [children] unto Molech shall surely be put to death. The people of the land shall stone him with stones. And I will set My face against that man and will cut him off from among his people because he has given of his seed unto Molech to defile My sanctuary and to profane My holy name." Lev. 20:1-3. Ezekiel spoke for God: "For when you offer your gifts, when you make your sons to pass through the fire, you pollute yourselves with all your idols." Ezek. 20:31.

Jeremiah 3:9 laments that they committed adultery with stones and trees. James 4:4 teaches us that friendship with the world is adultery.

God demanded their undivided, unadulterated worship and obedience to Him. The true worship of God requires that we lay down the wants of our old man nature of flesh and sin—that we deny Self in total abandonment to God.

GOD DIVORCED ISRAEL

Israel was regarded by God as His betrothed. Jer. 3:14. God was faithful to her, but she was repeatedly unfaithful to Him. She attempted fidelity, occasionally, and there were times of repentance and restoration. The good kings purged the temple of idolatry, but even they did not always complete the job. They consistently kept their high places.

Of Solomon it is written, "Solomon loved the LORD, walking in the statutes of David his father: only he sacrificed and burnt incense in high places." 1 Kings 3:3. Asa did what was right in the eyes of the Lord. He banished the sodomites from the land and removed the idols of his father; he removed his mother, Maachah, from being queen because she had made an idol in a grove; but "the high places were not removed." 1 Kings 15:11-14. "Jehoshaphat walked in all the ways of Asa his father, doing that which was right in the eyes of the LORD," but did not take away the high places. 1 Kings 22:43. Jehoash (2 Kings 12:1-3), Amaziah (2 Kings 14:1-4), Jeroboam (2 Kings 15:1-4),

---

[6]*Nelson's New Illustrated Bible Dictionary*, s.v. "Ashtoreth."

Uzziah and Jotham (2 Kings 15:32-34) likewise did what was right in the sight of the Lord except they did not take away the high places.

The scriptures tell us that Hezekiah and Josiah were the only Kings who removed even the high places. Hezekiah "did what was right in the sight of the LORD; according to all that David his father did. He removed the high places, and broke the images, and cut down the groves." 2 Kings 18:3-4a. The record says Josiah removed the high places "and like unto him was there no king before him, that turned to the LORD with all his heart, and with all his soul, and with all his might, according to all the law of Moses; neither after him arose there any like him." 2 Kings 23:25. But for these two, king after king had this one thing in common: they did not remove the high places.

During the days that Josiah was king, the Lord asked Jeremiah if he had seen what backsliding Israel had done. He said that she had gone up on every high mountain and under every green tree and played the harlot; and for all the causes for which backsliding Israel had committed adultery, God had her put away and given her a certificate of divorce. Jer. 3:6,8.

TAKEN CAPTIVE

Earlier in Israel's history, after Solomon's reign as king, the Kingdom of Israel divided. The kingdom of Israel (later called Samaria) consisted of the ten tribes to the north which split from the kingdom after the death of Solomon during the reign of his son Rehoboam. It was ruled by Jeroboam. The Kingdom of Judah consisted of the two remaining tribes in the south, Judah and Benjamin.

Through the prophet Ezekiel, God portrayed these two kingdoms as daughters of one mother. He gave these daughters the names Aholah and Aholibah. Aholah means "her own tent" and Aholibah means "women of the tent" or "the tent is in her." Aholah was the older daughter, Samaria, and Aholibah was the younger daughter, Judah (or Jerusalem). Ezekiel says, "...they committed whoredoms in Egypt; they committed whoredoms in their youth: their breasts were pressed there, and the teats of their virginity were bruised." Ezek. 23:3.

Though Aholah belonged to the Lord, she played the harlot and doted on her Assyrian lovers. She committed her whoredoms with them and defiled herself. So, God banished her into the hands of her lovers, the Assyrians.

Her sister, Aholibah, saw all that her older sister had done and how she had been taken away into captivity by her Assyrian lovers;

yet, she multiplied her whoredoms more than her sister.

God sent the Babylonians to take Judah away into captivity as a judgment against her. God said, "I will set My jealousy against you, and they shall deal furiously with you." Ezek. 23. Therefore, because of their idolatries and harlotries, Samaria was scattered to the nations by the Assyrians. Judah (Jerusalem) was taken into Babylonian captivity by the Babylonians.

The scriptures make it clear that these adulterous acts of idolatry were abominations to God. Ezekiel 16:51-52 reveals that Judah had committed twice the sins of her sister Samaria. She had multiplied her abominations.

Of all the sins Israel and Judah committed, idolatry was the most abominable to God. Their idolatry was the one thing that led to their downfall. They forsook God for their high places. We are no different today. We, too, have our high places and our high places are just as much a snare to us.

Chapter 5

Our High Places

I rarely saw Benny without hearing some piece of profound wisdom suitable to a sage. This day was no exception. With that typical twinkle in his eye and that wry west Tennessee grin on his face, he asked me, "Do you know how you can tell when something is an idol in your life?"

"No." I waited for his reply. I knew it would be good.

His grin widened. His words were slow but short. "By how big a fight you put up when it's taken from you."

Many of the things we fight over are likely idols in our lives. We get angry when something we adore is taken from us or when we fear that it might be taken from us.

OUR HIGH PLACES

We, as with Israel of old, have our idols. Our idols are our high places. Our high places are those things we cherish above our consecration to God. We, too, have gone "a whoring" after the gods of our own making. We "burn incense" to the work of our hands and the imaginations of our minds when we take self-exalted pride in our accomplishments. Such things as science, government, the stock market, religion, the arts, diets, entertainment, and sports can work for our good, but they become idolatrous when we put our trust in them rather than in God. We make ourselves out to be God.

This was the lie in the garden of Eden: if we could know as God knows, we would become as God. So we, in Adam, became knowledgeable, and that knowledge became a curse to us. We play God when we glory in our own intellectual abilities to figure things out, reason things, understand things, invent things, and imagine even greater achievements. We exalt that which we think we know above the knowledge of God. It keeps us at arms-length from God and prevents us from entering into intimacy with Father-God, our Creator. Puffed-up knowledge is the arrogance of Self, and Self is that high mountain upon which we build our altars.

EXTENSIONS OF SELF

Our high places are extensions of ourselves. We stand back like a master painter and survey the canvas of our works and sigh, "Ah! This is what *I* did!" Our identities are wrapped up in our achievements. We want to be somebody, to make our mark, to leave our fingerprint on something important. Our old man of flesh natures are driven by the need for power, position, recognition, possessions, and domination.

We bow the knee to those who are rich and famous, and snub, or at best patronize, those who are poor and uncelebrated. We, as Nimrod, have journeyed to our land of Shinar, looking to build a tower, a city, and a name for ourselves. Gen. 11. Those who have "Ministries" do this as well.

CHURCH AS AN EXTENSION OF SELF

This Thing we call *church* can be one such extension of ourselves. It is one of those things we go after in our hearts because we love *it* so. That is to say, we love the works of our hands and the imaginations of our hearts that are expressed in that Thing we call *church*. We are in *church* because *church* is in us. *It* is an extension of us. Therefore, we are serving ourselves when we serve *it*.

"Ah, come on," you say. "You can't be serious. Aren't you being too hard and critical of the *church*? I love my *church*. I have life-long relationships in my *church*. We have a great choir, good preaching, souls are saved, the Holy Spirit often moves in our services. The ritual and symbols make me feel close to God. How do you account for the fact that God shows up in *church*? How can you call *church* evil?"

Good Christian people go to *church*. In fact, the stronger they are in their faith, the more likely they are to go to *church*. They identify "going to *church*" with their faith. Their faithfulness to *church* is often the yardstick for measuring their faithfulness to Christ. After all, the *churches* even belong to Christians, at least in name and perception. God's presence is manifested in some of these *churches* on occasions, but none of this means that these Things we call *church* have been born of the Spirit. They are still idolatrous extensions of Self.

God often blessed and prospered His people in captivity. God blessed Israel on numerous occasions even though she was engaged in idolatry. Even when He banished Judah to Babylon, He commanded that they build houses, plant gardens, eat the fruit of them, and increase in families. Jer. 29:4-6. God even pronounced severe judgment against those idolatrous Jews who tried to stay behind in Judah. Jer. 29:16-18. "After seventy years are accomplished in Babylon," the Lord promised Judah, "I will visit you, and perform My good word toward you, in causing you to return to this place." Jer. 29:10. God had to visit His people in Babylon in order to deliver them from Babylon.

The Holy Spirit has often moved upon His people to save, heal, and deliver them throughout the history of the institutionalized *church* system. The Protestant reformation, the great awakening of the 1800's, and the Pentecostal revival of the 1900's are major historical examples of how God sought to deliver His people out of an old order to bring them into a new order.

A few *churches* have experienced what they call renewal. God is filling the lamps of those willing to be prepared with enough oil to go the distance when that last trumpet sounds. It would be a tragic mistake, however, to take God's anointing upon His people as an endorsement of their idols. If the Holy Spirit is moving in your *church*, He is not present to bless your idolatries, but to prepare a people unto Himself. God cares for His people who happen to be in captivity to *church*. He is preparing His bride. He has to go into these illegitimate places we call the *church* to prepare her so He can take her out.

THE BRIDE IN HARLOTRY

Bill Shipman saw it this way. "It was almost like a vision," he explained.

> I was there in the chambers and on the streets with them. I saw Jesus waiting in a groom's chamber. The bride was in another chamber. He was preparing to go in to see her. While He delayed, she was drawn to the window and became interested in the activities in the street. The appeal of the street tugged at her harlot heart until she wandered out there herself.
>
> Soon after she walked out onto the streets she was raped. Her shame deceived her into believing that she had no other life but to become a prostitute, which she did. She was in a house of prostitution, locked behind huge, solid-oak, medieval doors. They looked formidable. They were bolted through with a braided kind of thing with copper on it and different kinds of ironwork.
>
> Jesus went looking for her. He knew where she was. As He approached the doors, demons howled and hissed at Him and tried to rush Him, yet were cowardly toward Him. He

opened the doors and went in. She was really a mess, and He pleaded with her to come with Him. In her guilt and shame, she refused, and so He left.

He waited a time and visited her again. Still, she wouldn't look Him in the face. Once again, he left her. As He was waiting in His chamber, fires of passion and anger suddenly flashed in His eyes. He stormed out of His chamber and strode down the street, approaching the house where His bride in harlotry abided.

Everyone saw Him coming. They fled to get out of His way. The demons took one look at Him and ran ahead of Him to lock the doors, hoping to prevent Him from entering. Without hesitation or pause in his stride, He hit those doors with the palms of His hands. POW! They exploded. Splinters went everywhere.

He walked in and found her withered in shame. Her face was hidden in her hands. This time was different though. This time He didn't ask her to come with Him. This time He grasped her hand, led her out, and took her back to the bride's chamber while she was still in her filthy, semen-stained dress.

I could see the passion and love He had for her in His eyes. Jesus saw her only one way. He saw her as a virgin. Yet, she wouldn't even look at Him. He reached out, touched her gently, and lifted her face toward His. Hesitantly, she slowly lifted her eyes to look into His. He saw her beyond her shame and forced her beyond her shame. The moment her eyes connected with His, they were filled with the same passion for Him that He had for her.

I was right in there with them. I could almost see into their faces. I backed off and saw that she had changed. She was beautiful. She had the same radiance as did Jesus. They were one. There was no longing or attraction for anyone or anything other than for one another. She had eyes only for Him. She looked like Him, and He looked like her. They were standing in one light. He was not diminished at all, but she was increased in Him. Even though she looked like Him and had the same fire in her eyes as He had in His, she was still under His feet, still under His authority. That's what made it as beautiful as it was.

I believe Bill's vision is from the Lord and reveals perfectly how He sees His bride in harlotry and how He intends to come for us.

Indeed, even as His bride, we have played the harlot with our substitutes for Jesus. Perhaps even now we feel the shock waves of His footsteps coming near to rid us of our shame and dress us in robes of righteousness.

THE HIGH PLACE OF *CHURCH*

To substitute *church* for Jesus is idolatry in enormous proportions. We are not to lift up *church* and make it the way of salvation. Jesus alone is our salvation.

Many people have made an idol out of *church* just as the Israelites made an idol out of the serpent in the wilderness. When the people accused God and Moses of bringing them up out of Egypt to die in the wilderness, the Lord sent fiery serpents among them, and the serpents bit the people because of their grumbling. Many of the Israelites died. The people repented, and God relented. God told Moses to make a fiery serpent and set it upon a pole. All who had been bitten could look upon it and live. Num. 21:4-9.

That should have been the end of the story. But notice 2 Kings 18:4! Hezekiah had become King of Judah, and the Bible says that he did what was right in the sight of the Lord. "He removed the high places, broke the images, cut down the groves, *and broke in pieces the brazen serpent that Moses had made: for until those days the children of Israel burned incense to it.*" They took an act of God and made an idol out of it. In this same idolatrous spirit, people have turned the moves of God into the denominations they later adored.

That which we call *church* today is an idolatrous system of men's traditions which is spiritual harlotry. *Church* is what we do in addition to being who Christ has made us to be in Him. If what we call *church* can be incorporated, joined, named, referred to as *it*, and can be taken from us, then *it* is not the real thing. The true ekklesia is a corporate body of people who are born into it. They have taken only the name of Jesus because they are in a relationship with Him. That relationship cannot be taken from them.

If *church* is not the real thing, then *it* is a counterfeit. The problem with counterfeits is that they look deceptively like the real thing. *Church*, as a counterfeit, is presented and perceived as the real thing. Strangely enough, though, *it* does not even remotely look like the real thing. Nevertheless, we have been beguiled into believing that *it* is.

Many people burn the incense of self-adoration to all that is associated with this Thing we call *church*. They have made idols out of their doctrines, forms of government, heritages, programs, rituals, liturgies, buildings, Sunday morning services, going to *church*, budgets, personalities, the Sunday School, youth meetings, missionary guilds, men's meetings, annual bazaars and events—everything associated with *church*. They frolic around their corporate achievements: their cemeteries, denominations, Bible schools, nursing homes, children's homes, hospitals, missions, jail ministries, and prison ministries. These can be God-appointed ministries and worthy causes, but they become idolatrous when we operate them to make ourselves look good and feel godly. Busyness is not godliness. These institutions are often more about those who operate them than about the ones they seek to serve.

Many of these *church* Things were originally started to meet the needs of people but soon became ends within themselves. Many of the institutions have become profit-driven instead of service-driven. Jesus said, "The Sabbath was made for man, and not man for the Sabbath." Mark 2:27. We have reversed that saying. Now, it is as though we exist for the sake of *church* and not *church* for us.

Moreover, we may have the attitude about our *church* that it has the right stuff. If possible, we competitively build a bigger and better steeple house than the folks down the street. We plan our services and harbor the hope that we will have the best show in town. Some of us hype our praise and worship, our prayers, our preaching, and even our offerings to convince even ourselves, perhaps, that the Holy Spirit is upon us.

We may devise programs in the name of evangelism and market ourselves in such a way so as to corral more folks—to rope, throw, and brand them with our special mark, to clone them like us. Yet, we want to stand out from the other *churches* in town. We craft our creeds to distinguish ourselves from them. The names we give ourselves reflect our separateness from them. We sometimes even brag about our differences. A young man at a gathering of men sported a T-shirt which was likely intended to communicate an innocent but catchy phrase; nonetheless, it revealed this separatist notion. It read, "Vineyard Church: Experience the difference."

For many deceived hearts, their *church* is their plan of salvation, and we have about as many salvation plans as we have *churches*. We stress the necessity of *church* membership and regular attendance to *church* and thereby communicate the subtle message that we are saved by these Things. We are considered unscriptural if we do not go to *church*.

Many *churches* associate water baptism with membership in their *church*. Some denominations (cults) preach that you are lost unless you are a member their *church*. For some, acceptance into their fold involves strict adherence to their rigid code of behavior.

For others, acceptance involves strict adherence to their rigid doctrine. "We have the right doctrine. Agree with us and be baptized into our *church*, and you will be saved." How absolutely ludicrous. Is not Jesus our Savior?

We have raised up shrines for ourselves, and we have become our own corpses within them. We have enshrined ourselves with a grandeur we seek for ourselves. There is no life in these shrines nor can there ever be. There is no hope of resurrection life within them for they exist to provide something for Self. Resurrection life comes through the denial of oneself and not to those who seek to save themselves.

OUR IDOLATRY IS SPIRITUAL HARLOTRY

When the bride plays the harlot, she becomes one with the harlot, and distinguishing between the bride and her harlotries becomes difficult. If you play the harlot, you become the harlot. The apostle Paul wrote, "Know you not that your bodies are the members of Christ? Shall I then take the members of Christ, and make them the members of a harlot? God forbid. What? Know you not that he who is joined to a harlot is one body? For two, says He, shall be one flesh. But he who is joined unto the Lord is one spirit." 1 Cor. 6:15-17.

Paul was writing to Corinthian believers who were, with all saints in all places and in all times, the bride of Christ. A bride is feminine in gender. A harlot is feminine in gender. I mean no disparagement against anyone who is sexually broken, but when the bride of Christ joins herself to the harlotry of Self, she is operating in the perverse spirit of spiritual lesbianism and practicing spiritual self-sex. We are more "in lust" with ourselves than we are in sacrificial relationship with our Bridegroom, the Lord Jesus Christ. He is jealous of that.

STRONGHOLDS OF THE MIND

These idolatries of Self are strongholds of the mind. A spiritual stronghold is the preoccupation with an object, a person, or an institution; with anger or fear; with a fetish, an addiction, or a sin. A spiritual stronghold is anything that fascinates us, dominates our minds, and causes us to behave obsessively and compulsively. These are things that rule over us. We seem powerless to do anything about them. Yet, we cannot deny that these things are harmful to us or others.

A spiritual stronghold can also be the grid through which we see things. *Church* is one such stronghold of the mind. We have been brainwashed into believing that *church* as we know and practice it is what we ought to do. We have never known anything other than *church* as we practice *it*. So, when I say *church* is an idol and a stronghold in your mind, you may have a difficult time believing it. You cannot see it. Even if you see it, you have a hard time accepting it because of your programmed mind-set. Once you see the deception, however, receive the truth, and begin to walk in that light, you find your mind changing. The stronghold is being torn down.

Taking the bride of Christ out of *church* is not an easy matter, because *church* is a stronghold in her mind. God has to take *church* out of us, as well as take us out of *it*. Strange language is it not? For while God is trying to take us out of *church*, we are trying to get people into *it*. If we try to leave the stronghold of *church* before it has been taken out of us, we will simply return to *it*.

Christmas. Christmas is one of those strongholds of the mind. It had not been celebrated in any form before the third century. Alexander Hislop explains, "Long before the fourth century, and long before the Christian era itself, a festival was celebrated among the *heathen*, at that precise time of the year, in honor of the birth of the son of the Babylonian queen of heaven; and it may fairly be presumed that, in order to conciliate the heathen, and to swell the number of the nominal adherents of Christianity, the same festival was adopted by the Roman Church, giving it only the name of Christ."[7] They took this strictly pagan celebration and put Jesus in the center of it.

Rome instituted a mass which was called Christ-mass—shortened to Christmas. Christmas has always been, is now, and ever shall be a pagan festival. It has grown over the centuries to become the enchanting, magical, merchant-driven insult to God that it now is. We are mesmerized by it. Hooked on it. Enslaved by it. In debt to it. Dennis Loewen adds, "Christmas is another example of how powerful the false *living* spirit of harlotry is. There is a spirit of Christmas. It is warm; it is wonderful; it is good...and it is not from God."

The world loves Christmas as much as Christians do. What does that tell us? One "Christian" celebrity said on national TV that Christmas is three things: "decorating, gift-giving, and eating." We must know that what the world loves cannot be of God. The apostle John exhorts us, "Love not the world, neither the things that are in the world. If any man loves the world, the love of the Father is not in him. For all that is in the world, the lust of the flesh, and the lust

---

[7]Alexander Hislop, *The Two Babylons or The Papal Worship* (Neptune, NJ: Loizeaux Brothers, 1959), 93. Hislop's book is quite exhaustive, well documented, and convincing.

of the eyes, and the pride of life, is not of the Father, but is of the world." 1 John 2: 15-16.

The fact that most of what people do at Christmas has its roots in this pagan mid-winter festival should be reason enough for Christians not to do it—the tree and lights, the candles, the mistletoe, the exchange of gifts, the yule log in the fireplace, the cakes, the goose, the drunkenness, and even the date of December the 25th. The fact that this season is so merchant-driven today should add to our disdain for it. However, the real slap-in-the-face to God is that we love these soulish things more than obedience to Him. They are emotional strongholds in our minds. We would lack sound judgment to believe that we can relentlessly celebrate these days and seasons and stay free of their captivation.

The idea of not celebrating Christmas carries such an affront to others that most people could not give it up even if they were convinced that it was an abomination to God. We are thought leprous for not going along with it. We are pleasers of men rather than of God.

I have heard the cliché since my childhood to "put Christ back into Christmas." It is often inscribed this way: "Put Christ back into X-mas." Even though the X probably stands for the Greek letter *chi* in *Chr*ist, we tend to think of it as X-ing out Jesus. Well, for years I have been thinking it and now I dare to say it: Instead of putting Jesus back into a pagan festival where He never belonged in the first place, let us take Him out of it altogether and give it back to the world to whom it belongs. After all, the Bible never called for this celebration, and Jesus would never impose such crazy-making bondage upon us. Paul wrote, "It was for freedom that Christ set us free; therefore keep standing firm and do not be subject again to a yoke of slavery." Gal. 5:1 NAS. This is what we should teach our children.

Christmas is one of those "high places" that most of us seem unwilling to tear down, even knowing how God might feel about it. Our minds are made up. "I like Christmas," one young mother told me. The rest of her sentence was implied, "So I'm going to do it." We build manger scenes in our yards and erect glow-in-the-dark Santa Clauses next to them. Buddy at the checkout counter illustrated this mix very simply. He had a Santa Claus hat on his head and a W.W.J.D. (what would Jesus do?) band around his neck. Buddy, Jesus would not have worn that hat.

After I told a dear old lady why I no longer do Christmas, she responded, "But I don't think of pagan gods when I look at my Christmas tree. I think of Jesus." That seemed reasonable to me. I asked God about it. He answered. "What would you think if you caught your wife in adultery, and she answered, 'But, honey, I was thinking of you the whole time'?"

Many people reason, "we do it for the children." If Christmas is idolatrous for the parents, then why would the parents want to sacrifice their children to these idols?

Easter. Easter is equally idolatrous and chilling. Most Christians affectionately use the term Easter in association with the precious resurrection of our Lord Jesus Christ with no regard to the fact that Easter is the English word for the goddess Ishtar (also called Astarte and Eostre in other pagan cultures). Ishtar was celebrated as the queen of heaven. Much of what we do at Easter time also has its origin in paganism. The date on which we celebrate Easter does not regularly coincide with the resurrection of Christ, which occurred three days after Passover. Lent, the sunrise services, the dyeing of eggs, the bunny rabbits are all unscriptural abominations to God.

So, how did we come to do those things? Alexander Hislop writes, "To conciliate the Pagans to nominal Christianity, Rome, pursuing its usual policy, took measures to get the Christian and Pagan festivals amalgamated, and, by a complicated but skillful adjustment of the calendar, it was found no difficult matter, in general, to get Paganism and Christianity—now far sunk in idolatry—in this as in so many other things, to shake hands."[8]

Dennis Loewen observes, "The harlot isn't picky about these things. She will lay down with anything as long as it is another Jesus. She reasons, 'Why bother with these details?' God, on the other hand, does mind. How could anyone read the scriptures and see Him otherwise?"

EMPOWERING OUR HIGH PLACES

We empower those things we bow down and pay homage to. We release God's power in our lives when we bow down and worship Him. Likewise, we empower our idols when we bow down to them whether they are men, buildings, institutions, ideas, science, opinions, demons, or that Thing we call *church*.

Patrick came to town to start a new *church*. As is often the case, the Lord's anointing was present, and people freely entered into praise and worship. Relationships were forming. The vision seemed, at first, to be targeted toward building up the people into Christ. There was liberty. Then came the desire for a building, then

---

[8]Hislop, p.105.

the need for a loan, then the need for more money, and finally a drive for membership. The people found themselves drawn back into that which they had tried to come out of. Patrick was taking them back into what he came out of, because what he had come out of had never been taken out of him. Instead of building a people, he was consumed with building a *church*—his *church*. A few discerning people who went to his *church* left when they realized that staying served only to endorse and empower his idolatry.

We empower the idolatry of *church* when we attend *its* services.

We empower the idolatry of *church* when we contribute to *it*.

We empower the idolatry of *church* when we insist upon using the term *church* in reference to the body of Christ.

We empower the idolatry of *church* when we ask one another where we go to *church?*

We empower the idolatry of *church* when we measure other people's spirituality by where they *go* to *church*.

We have our high places; yet, we know God's heart in such matters because He clearly told us, "You shall have no other gods before Me." Exod. 20:3.

The Holy Spirit may lead a mature, liberated believer to attend a *church* and perhaps contribute to *it* for a purpose known only to God and that believer. If, however, that believer becomes joined in his heart to that system, once again lifting it up, he has returned to the idolatry and spiritual harlotry of *it*. He is deceived. One who feels called of God to stay in or return to one of those harlot *church* system situations has to be honest with himself regarding his true motive lest he say, "God told me to" in order to justify the harlot desires of his heart.

AUGURING OUT THE IDOLATRY

For the most part, first century believers went from house to house which may be an ideal plan for gathering even today. More and more believers in relationship are being drawn into each other's living rooms for praise and worship, sharing the word, breaking bread, prayer, and fellowship. These settings can provide tremendous liberty in the Holy Spirit, create opportunities for each one to use his or her gifts, draw them closer together in relationships, and maintain support for one another in times of need.

However, we must understand that our salvation does not depend upon meeting in home groups anymore than belonging to *church*. Our salvation is in the Lord. We can make an idolatrous thing out of home groups just as easily as we can out of *church*. The problem is not in having a building or not, having regular meetings or not, having programs or not, or having structure or not. The problem has to do with what is in our hearts about those things. It may be possible to have all of those things and not become joined to them, though I doubt it. Sooner or later, without realizing it, we make a Thing of them and begin go after the Thing rather than the Lord. That is how our harlot hearts work. For, after all, those things came out of our hearts. I think it is most unlikely that we can organize ourselves as a group of believers with a building, a name, a bank account, belief system, and such without those things sooner or later becoming a source of pride in us as idolatrous extensions of our fleshly need to exalt Self.

I find that there is a mix in many *churches*. There is both flesh and Spirit because, until now, God has responded to His people wherever they call upon His name. He responds in spite of the fact that we have made these Things idols in our lives. He responds to the Holy Spirit and His nature within us. Nevertheless, He despises our flesh and our idolatries. I dare not touch what God is doing in any person or *church*. I desire only to augur out the idolatrous part of it all and expose our harlot hearts that we might repent of that.

If you are in one of those Things we call *church* and are truly growing in the Lord, I would not want to say leave it physically, but abandon any idolatry of it. And beware! Phil Perry observed that "the more the Holy Spirit seems to be moving in one of those Things, the more deceiving it is. People see all that God is doing, and fail to see all the things that are wrong." The "things that are wrong" are terribly wrong. The snare is still set to trap you and engage you as a slave to the system for life. Many groups may have begun in the Spirit, but are continuing on in the flesh. Gal. 3:3.

We are to be a people who are led by the Holy Spirit in all that we do, say, and are. We are to worship Him in spirit and truth. Anything, including *church*, that hinders us from doing so cannot be from God.

Our high places are our Babylonian lovers, and *church* is the modern day Babylonian captivity of God's people.

Chapter 6

Spiritual Babylon

*W*hat is spiritual Babylon today? Opinions rival one another.

Alexander Hislop argues that the woman in Revelation 17 said to be "sitting on seven mountains," and having on her forehead the name written, "Mystery, Babylon the Great," is associated with the Roman apostasy [the Roman Catholic Church].[9] Others are of the opinion that Babylon is the whole world system which is under the domain of Satan. A friend of mine has a convincing argument from scripture that the United States of America is modern Babylon. An internationally recognized prophet in our time has said that New York City is modern Babylon.

I say that Babylon is all of the above, yet more. Babylon was once a city in Mesopotamia. It has been spiritualized in the scriptures as something that is in contradiction to God. It is now a type of something spiritual. Babylon is not the Roman Catholic Church, but is a type of something often found in the Roman Catholic Church. Babylon is not the United States of America, but is a type of something in the United States of America. Babylon is not New York City, but is a type of something in New York City. Babylon certainly is not the body of Christ, but is a type of something in the hearts of many in the body—something that ought not to be there.

As I defined in chapter one, *Babylon is all that the carnal mind of man devises in the exaltation of Self—the preeminence of Self over God* whether in nations, cities, politics, government, science, technology, religion, philosophy, psychology, sociology, commerce, education, entertainment, or *church*. It is all that is in the world and of the world. It describes the spiritual condition of the *church*.

THE CARNAL MIND

Spiritual Babylon is primarily characterized by the idolatry of the carnal mind. Carnal is another word for the flesh. "Flesh" often refers to that fallen sin nature of man that is at enmity with God. The carnal mind is all thought, reason, logic, imagination, opinion, and speculation that is associated with the old Adamic mind of

---

[9]Hislop, p. 1.

fallen man. We practice Babylon when we do things according to our notion rather than God's.

The apostle Paul explained that those who do things according to the flesh, set their minds on the things of the flesh; but those who do according to the Spirit, set their minds on the things of the Spirit. "For to be carnally [fleshly] minded is death; but to be spiritually minded is life and peace. Because the carnal mind is enmity against God..." Rom. 8:5-7a.

The appeal in the garden was for Adam and Eve to exercise the power of their God-given intellect to elevate themselves in their own minds. God told Adam that he could eat from all of the trees in the garden except one. He was not to eat from the tree of the knowledge of good and evil. "For in the day that you eat thereof," God warned, "you shall surely die." Gen. 2:16-17. This ban was clear and simple. God said what He meant and meant what He said. That should have settled it.

Satan, however, slithered onto the limb of their intellect and reasoned, "You shall not surely die: for God knows that in the day you eat thereof, your eyes shall be opened, and you shall be as gods, knowing good and evil." Gen. 3:4-5. Knowing good and evil was an appeal to the idolatry of the mind. Once they yielded to the temptation and ate of the fruit, their minds became fleshly. They were transformed into a nature that was different from the way God created them.

Genesis 3:6 tells us three things about Eve: She saw that the fruit of the tree was good for food, that it was pleasant to the eyes, and desirable to make one wise. This verse also tells us that God created man with the ability to make choices, with the desire to be like God, and with the vulnerability to be deceived. Eve was enticed with the prospect of having knowledge and being equal to God. So, she bit into the lie and gave it to her husband to eat of it also. Gen. 3:6.

The ability to make choices is not a sin. It is a gift from God. We sin when we make choices contrary to God's will. We think we know better than God. Therefore, we exalt our knowledge, logic, reasoning, opinions, imaginations, speculations, and every other high-minded thing above the knowledge of God. 2 Cor. 10:5. We ignore that part of God's word that does not agree with our aspirations, expectations, theologies, and doctrines. We believe what we want to believe. We foolishly make ourselves out to be God. We even make up God to be the way we want Him to be. Thus, we are in rebellion against God just as Adam and Eve were.

Paul wrote against the arrogance of knowledge saying, "If a man thinks himself to be something, when he is nothing, he deceives himself." Gal 6:3. Again he wrote, "If anyone supposes that he knows anything, he has not yet known as he ought to know." 1 Cor. 8:2 NAS.

DECEPTION

Spiritual Babylon is characterized by deception. Satan deceived Eve. He implied that God had lied to them. If, indeed, they ate of the tree of the knowledge of good and evil, Satan argued, they would become like God, knowing good and evil.

Eve believed Satan's lies and immediately structured her own false reality around those lies. She incorporated those lies into her paradigm of reality. She constructed her own truth about God and sighed, "Oh, I see now!" Rather than having her eyes opened, however, she actually became spiritually blind.

Before they went in to possess the land of Canaan, God warned the Israelites to guard their hearts lest they be *deceived*. Deut. 11:16. Paul wrote, "Let no man *deceive* himself. If any man among you seems to be wise in this world, let him become a fool, that he may be wise." 1 Cor. 3:18. He charged his readers several times not to be deceived. 1 Cor. 6:9; 15:33; Gal. 6:7. To the Ephesians he wrote, "Let no man *deceive* you with vain words." Eph. 5:6. To the Colossians he wrote, "Beware lest any man spoil you through philosophy and vain *deceit*, after the traditions of men, and not after Christ." Col. 2:8. To the Thessalonians he wrote, "Let no man *deceive* you by any means." 2 Thess. 2:3. We can be blinded to the truth by lust, pleasures, malice, envy, and hate. Titus 3:3. We can be hardened by the deceitfulness of sin. Heb. 3:13. We can deceive ourselves by being hearers only of the word and not doers. James 1:22. We can deceive ourselves by being religious. James 1:26; 1 John 1:8. John adds: "Little children, let no man *deceive* you." 1 John 3:7. With this battery of scriptures in mind, do you believe we can possibly be deceived, even as believers in Christ? "For many *deceivers* have entered into the world, who confess not that Jesus Christ is come in the flesh. This is a *deceiver* and an antichrist." 2 John 1:7.

Hosea spoke for God saying, "Hear the word of the LORD, you children of Israel: for the LORD has a controversy with the inhabitants of the land, because there is no truth, nor mercy, nor knowledge of God in the land...My people are destroyed for lack of knowledge [of God]: because you have rejected knowledge [of God]." Hos. 4:1,6a. Spiritual Babylon—all that the carnal mind devises—is the exaltation of what we construct as truth over what God says is truth.

PRIDE

Spiritual Babylon is characterized by pride. The prideful nature of Self thinks it knows. It thinks it knows better than God. It makes decisions all day, every day without consulting God, without even asking for wisdom. When smitten with pride, we are lifted up in who we think we are and what we think we know. Self is prideful, arrogant, and haughty. "Knowledge puffs up." 1 Cor. 8:1.

Spiritual Babylon is associated with the arrogance of those who followed Nimrod to the land of Shinar (Babel).[10] The Bible says they were of one language and one speech and said to one another, "'Let us make brick, and burn them thoroughly.' And they had brick for stone, and they had slime for mortar. And they said, 'Let us build us a city and a tower, whose tip may reach heaven; and let us make a name for ourselves'." Gen. 11: 3-4.

Churches and ministries are snared by the prideful temptation to gather larger numbers of people, build bigger buildings with steeples pointing to heaven, and make names for themselves, succumbing to the temptation to exalt Self. We name our *churches*, ministries, and institutions after ourselves. We dedicate stained-glass windows and pews in memory of men. We put our names on things for self-glory.

What a contrast to those who follow Jesus! As Paul exhorted, "Let this mind be in you, which was also in Christ Jesus who, being in the form of God, thought it not robbery to be equal with God, but made Himself of no reputation, and took upon Him the form of a servant, and was made in the likeness of men. And being found in fashion as a man, He humbled himself, and became obedient unto death, even the death of the cross." Phil. 2:5-8.

EXALTED SELF

Spiritual Babylon is characterized by the exaltation of Self. The exalted Self says, "I can save, heal, deliver, and fix myself." "I will increase my knowledge in science, my power in politics, my performance in religion, my investments in the marketplace, my insights into the psyche of man." "I will alter the genetics of humans, clone humans, abort babies, and change the laws so I will feel comfortable doing these things." "I will become an entertainer, rock star, model, sports superstar, politician, writer, musician, or televangelist in order to achieve fame and fortune." "I can build a *church* around my revelations, my teachings, and my programs by which I imply that others can be saved, healed, and delivered."

---

[10]Shinar was that territory that later became known as Babylon. Babel is the Hebrew name for Babylon.

This is the spirit of the king of Babylon in our hearts which Isaiah calls Lucifer (meaning "light-bearer"—the name also given to Satan). He is the one of whom Isaiah writes: "How are you fallen from heaven, O Lucifer, son of the morning! How are you cut down to the ground, which weakened the nations! For you have said in your heart, '*I* will ascend into heaven. *I* will exalt my throne above the stars of God. *I* will sit also upon the mount of the congregation, in the sides of the north. *I* will ascend above the heights of the clouds. *I* will be like the most High.' Yet you shall be brought down to hell, to the sides of the pit." Isa. 14:12-15. "I," "I," "I."

The King of Babylon, Nebuchadnezzar, walked in the palace of his kingdom and said, "Is not this great Babylon, that I have built for the house of the kingdom by the might of my power, and for the honor of my majesty?" Dan. 4:30. We who lift ourselves up like King Nebuchadnezzar will be brought down like King Nebuchadnezzar. "While the word was in the king's mouth, there fell a voice from heaven, saying, 'O King Nebuchadnezzar, to you it is spoken; The kingdom is departed from you.'" Dan. 4:31. He was driven from men to dwell in the field with the beasts where he ate grass as oxen do, possibly for seven years. This happened to him that he might come to know that the most High God rules in the kingdom of men and gives kingdoms to whomever He will. Dan. 4:32.

We have believed the lie of the serpent in the garden; we believe that we are our own god. How pathetic! We get so joined to this lie that it is perceived as truth and as something to be desired. We esteem ourselves over God.

Jesus said, "Whosoever shall exalt himself shall be abased; and he who humbles himself shall be exalted." Matt. 23:12.

CONFUSION

Spiritual Babylon is characterized by confusion. Babel means confusion. Gen. 11:9. The Lord saw that the settlers in Shinar were one people and spoke one language which meant, according to God's own words, that nothing would be held from them that they imagined to do. Thereupon, God said, "Let us go down, and there confound [confuse] their language, that they may not understand one another's speech." Gen. 11:7. The Lord scattered them to all parts of the earth so that they were not able to finish building their city.

Everything that is in the world continues to be marked by confusion. We have confusion among nations, confusion among ethnic groups, confusion in government, confusion in the economic marketplace, confusion in education, confusion in science and technology, confusion in the home, and confusion in the local *church*.

Because Christians have refused to follow the leading of the Holy Spirit and have insisted upon building their own little towers to heaven, we have great diversity, disunity, and confusion among us. If we find ourselves in confusion, something other than or in addition to God is talking to us. The carnal mind is in operation and in opposition to the Spirit of God.

James says: "For where envying and strife is, there is *confusion* and every evil work." James 3:16. If we have the mind of Christ, we will be of one mind. If we are not of one mind, one or all of us are wallowing in the slime of the carnal mind. When we, as God's people, however, seek His will, He will not cause us to be in confusion. God is not the author of confusion. 1 Cor. 14:33.

IMAGINATIONS

Spiritual Babylon is characterized by vain imaginations. God said of those in Babel that "nothing will be restrained from them, which they have *imagined* to do." Gen. 11:6. They were building unto themselves by their own hands with brick and slime what they had imagined in their minds.

The ability to imagine, as with the ability to reason and make choices is a God-given virtue. Imaginations are not evil in and of themselves. They become evil when we glory in them and glory in those things we invent as the result of them. We can accomplish spectacular things with the work of our hands from the imaginations of our minds. We walk the moon and put land-rovers on Mars. We pack gigabytes of memory onto tiny computer chips. We surf infinite miles on the information superhighway of the World Wide Web. We dwarf the great pyramids of Egypt with our modern skyscrapers. One person in the right place with the wrong mind-set can push a button and annihilate large cities in minutes.

By the same powers of intellect and imagination, we can build mega-ministries, universities, cathedrals, and circle the globe with "Christian television" and "Christian programming." We do what appears to be "mighty exploits for God" in the arm of self-strength. Nothing seems impossible to us if we can only imagine it.

Mary said of Jesus while He was yet in her womb: "He has scattered the proud in the imagination of their hearts." Luke 1:51. Paul wrote regarding the unrighteous that "they glorified Him not as God, neither were thankful; but became vain in their imaginations, and their foolish hearts were darkened." Rom. 1:21.

We are to cast "down imaginations and every high thing that exalts itself against the knowledge of God," and bring "into captivity every thought to the obedience of Christ." 2 Cor. 10:5. Unless our works are inspired of God, they will not withstand the fire of God. They are wood, hay, and stubble. 1 Cor. 3:11;15.

BABBLE

Spiritual Babylon is characterized by babble. Babble is useless chatter. "In the multitude of words sin is not lacking, but he who restrains his lips is wise." Prov. 10:19 NKJV. Words, words, words. Have you heard it said of some people that they babble on and on? Their words are often senseless, boring, and toxic. They talk when they need to be listening. They answer before they hear. Of such, Proverbs 18:13 says, "He who answers a matter before he hears it, it is folly and shame to him." Such people are said to have no ears.

Proverbs pictures the wordiness of Babylon in these verses: "He who opens wide his lips shall have destruction." Prov. 13:3. "In the mouth of the foolish is a rod of pride." Prov. 14:3. "Idle chatter leads only to poverty." Prov. 14:23 NKJV. "The mouth of fools pours out foolishness." Prov. 15:2. "A fool's lips enter into contention, and his mouth calls for strokes. A fool's mouth is his destruction, and his lips are the snare of his soul. The words of a talebearer are as wounds, and they go down into the innermost parts of the belly." Prov. 18:6-8. "See a man who is hasty in his words? There is more hope for a fool than for him." Prov. 29:20.

Some people talk and never say anything. Some people talk until they say something. Rare are those who talk only when they have something to say. Peter wrote, "If any man speak, let him speak as the oracles of God..." 1 Pet. 4:11. Would not that be the day!?

ACCUMULATION OF KNOWLEDGE

Spiritual Babylon is characterized by the accumulation of knowledge. The extremely rapid increase of knowledge in this present day is foretold in Daniel 12:4: "Conceal these words and seal up the book until the end of time; many will go back and forth and knowledge will increase."

The time in which we live has been classified as The Information Age. Knowledge mushrooms. Every new piece of knowledge multiplies what we learn. There seems to be no limit to the knowledge we can accumulate today. There seems to be no limit to what we humans can do with the knowledge we accumulate. Because of what we know, new thresholds in space are constantly crossed with each succeeding launch. Computers and computer programs are outdated by the time they hit the market. Major surgery is performed without intrusive incisions. High-tech wars can be won in a matter of days. Knowledge becomes more powerful than money.

We rely upon our own abilities to research, explore, examine, know, understand, and discover things. We have an insatiable appetite for more knowledge, to pull things up by the roots to see what they are made of. We have become a society of technomaniacs. We presume that we can solve our own problems with more knowledge.

Knowledge is one of our Babylons, one of our high places, and we are the god we worship. Knowledge that leads to self-idolatry is the tree of the *knowledge* of good and evil. Every year men and women graduate from seminaries by the thousands to fill pulpits around the world. There they will apply the higher-critical and near atheistic interpretations of the scriptures which they learned. They are spiritually bankrupted by such high-minded learning and are spiritually bankrupting their parishioners. Paul would have the same fear today that he had for the Corinthians: "But I fear, lest by any means, as the serpent beguiled Eve through his subtlety, so your minds should be corrupted from the simplicity that is in Christ." 2 Cor. 11:3.

SECTARIANISM

Spiritual Babylon is characterized by sectarianism.

After the people in the land of Shinar purposed in their hearts to build a city, a tower, and a name for themselves, the Lord came down and said, "Indeed the people are one and they all have one language, and this is what they begin to do; now nothing that they propose to do will be withheld from them. Come, let Us go down and there confuse their language, that they may not understand one another's speech." The place was called Babel because the Lord confused their language and moved them to all parts of the world. Gen. 11:2-9.

Because this Thing we call *church* is of the flesh and is an aspect of spiritual Babylon, *it* is under this same curse of confusion and sectarianism. *It* is founded on sectarianism, even thrives on it. *It* promotes the disunity of the body of Christ. *Its* very existence depends upon how each *church* system differs one from the other. This is easily seen in how their names billboard their differences.

Sectarianism says, "I am of Paul, I am of Apollos." Paul accused the Corinthian believers of being "fleshly" and "mere men" because of their sectarianism. There was jealousy and strife among them. They put their identity in personalities (Paul, Apollos, Cephas) rather than in the person of Jesus Christ. Apollos and Paul were both servants of the same Jesus. One planted; the other watered; but it was God who caused the growth. The one who plants and waters is nothing, but God is the One who matters because He causes the growth. When we understand that we are all fellow workers, God's field, God's building, then sectarianism will be edged out of the way. Disunity in the body turns into unity, oneness. There can only be one foundation, Jesus Christ. If what we have is sectarian and contributes to the disunity of the body, it has been built upon the wrong foundation. 1 Cor. 2.

Once we see this truth, we should have no need ever to name ourselves in order to identify what we are about. We are all about the Father's business, allowing the Holy Spirit who dwells in us to build us up as the temple of the Holy Spirit. "If any man defiles the temple of God, him shall God destroy; for the temple of God is holy, which temple you are." 1 Cor. 3:17. The more we separate ourselves within the body of Christ, the more we destroy the temple of the Holy Spirit.

RELIGION

Spiritual Babylon is characterized by religion. Even though masses of people seem to abhor religion of any kind, our sinful nature has a bent toward it because it is under the curse of condemnation and works. The first Adam was driven from the presence of God (condemnation) and told that he had to till the land and eat his bread in the sweat of his face (works). Gen. 3:19,23. Because the fallen man of flesh and sin is under the curse, he feels shame and wants to do something to make himself feel okay. Pagan man made up gods and then made up rituals (religious things to do) to try to appease their gods. Some of them even fed infant children to these gods of their own making.

Even though many people may be truly redeemed of the Lord, they still bring their shame-based flesh tendencies over into the life of the *church;* they know of only one way to relate to God, that is, through religion. Religiously inclined people love religion. It does not matter from one end of the spectrum to the other how people choose to express themselves religiously. Religion is still religion.

They love the religious atmosphere of *church* because *it* gives them something to do to salve the guilt of condemnation. Many well-meaning Christians are unaware that they go to *church* and do religious things out of a false sense of duty. They go because it makes them feel good. Perhaps they have not fully comprehended that there is "now no condemnation to them who are in Christ Jesus, who walk not after the flesh, but after the Spirit." Rom. 8:1.

Religion is foreign to God. He requires no religious thing of us. We are made spiritual beings by the presence and power of His Holy Spirit dwelling in us. His presence and power in us causes us to be and do what the Father requires of us. There is no way we can be righteous without it being His righteousness at work within us. That is why it is called grace. "For by grace are you saved through faith; and that not of yourselves: it is the gift of God: Not of works, lest any man should boast. For we are his workmanship, created in Christ Jesus unto good works, which God has before ordained that we should walk in them." Eph. 2:8-10. Religion stinks in the nostrils of God because it keeps us from having intimate relationships with Him. Our relationship is with our religion or with our *church*.

Flesh man deceives himself into thinking that if his religion makes him feel good, it must be good; therefore, he goes on doing his religious things. For such a one, *church* is often the religious thing he does. Yet, at the end of the day, after all is said and done, nothing is any different in him than it was before he engaged in that religious activity. He is just as empty on the inside as he was before. An abiding relationship with the Father through Jesus Christ is the only food that fills the soul to satisfaction.

RELIGIOUS SYSTEMS

The religious systems that make up and govern that Thing we call *church* characterize spiritual Babylon. Just as Judah and Jerusalem were once in Babylonian captivity, so are God's people today who are joined to *church* in their hearts. The brick and slime are the sectarian doctrines, creeds, traditions, festivals and celebrations, liturgies, rituals, lectionaries, polities, heritages, and ecclesiastical calendars. These things stand in place of or alongside a personal, living, dynamic relationship with God. These things that govern *church* have little to do with the Kingdom of God.

Most of us were born and raised in spiritual Babylon and have never known anything else. We have never seen what the body of Christ looks like as a pure and holy bride. Even though we know that all is not well within what we call *church*, we think that *it* can be fixed or at least made better, but *it* cannot.

THE ABOMINATION THAT MAKES DESOLATE

The rebellious carnal mind—immersed in deception, pride, the exaltation of Self, confusion, imaginations, babble, the accumulation of knowledge, sectarianism, religion, and its religious systems—is in the *church* as well as in the world. The abomination that makes desolate the holy place of God's temple of whom we are as believers, is rule of the carnal mind over obedience to God.

Jesus talked about this. While picturing the signs of the end to

His disciples, He mentioned the abomination of desolation which had been spoken of by Daniel the prophet. He told them that when they saw the abomination of desolation standing in the holy place they were to take various actions. (Read Matt. 24:15 and Mark 13:14.)

The abomination that makes desolate is described by Daniel for a future time. Dan. 12:9-11. Daniel was told that a vile person shall arise, muster forces, defile the sanctuary fortress, take away the daily sacrifices, and place there the abomination of desolation. Dan. 11:21-31 NKJV.

Some believe Daniel's prophecy was fulfilled around 165 B.C. when Antiochus IV (Epiphanes), Greek ruler of Syria, did the unthinkable. He sacrificed an unclean pig on the holy altar of the Jewish Temple. Others believe it was fulfilled when the Romans destroyed the Temple in 70 A.D. Still others suggest it will be fulfilled when the "man of sin" takes over the Temple and forces people to bow down to him, making himself to be like God.[11]

All of these suggestions point to natural, historical events. Perhaps it was or will be one of them. Perhaps it has multiple fulfillments and includes all of them. Consider, nonetheless, that what is generally expressed in the natural is also fulfilled in the spiritual realm. The New Testament writers explained that the spiritual is not first, but the natural; the spiritual follows the natural. 1 Cor 15:46; Heb. 9:11.

Jesus placed this abomination of desolation event in the future, even as a sign of the end times. Paul's writings agree that it was for a time future to his. 2 Thess. 2:3-4. Matthew indicated that the reader would need understanding. Matt. 24:15.

Consider that the body of Christ is spiritual Israel and the temple of the Holy Spirit. Where, then, would the abomination that makes the holy place desolate take place? It would take place within the minds and spirits of members of the body of Christ. We have already established from scriptures that it is possible for believers to be deceived.

The abomination occurs when the carnal mind is given precedence over the word of God and the mind of Christ. When we allow that, the holy place of our spirits is made desolate. When we bow down to those idolatrous systems of men's traditions as enshrined in our *churches*, we allow the abomination into the holy place which is our spirits. Our idolatries pollute the temple of the Holy Spirit. The carnal mind rules.

---

[11] *Nelson's New Illustrated Bible Dictionary*, s.v. "abomination of desolation."

THE FALL OF BABYLON

This Babylonian *church* will fall just as did historical Babylon.

Historical Babylon was used by God to judge Judah for her idolatries. Isa. 10:5-6. Daniel called Judah's judgment in Babylon a time of indignation (wrath). Dan. 11:36. When that seventy-year period of God's indignation was accomplished, God brought judgment against Babylon. Jer. 25:12. God prophesied to Babylon through Isaiah saying, "I was angry with My people, I profaned My heritage, and gave them into your hand. You did not show mercy to them." Isa. 47:6, NKJV.

God notes Babylon's pride: "Now, then hear this, you sensual one, who dwells securely, who says in your heart, I am, and there is no one besides me. I shall not sit as a widow, nor shall I know loss of children." Isa. 47:8.

He predicts what is going to happen to her: "Sit silently and go into darkness...For you will no more be called the queen of kingdoms...These two things shall come upon you suddenly in one day: loss of children and widowhood. They shall come on you in full measure in spite of your many sorceries, in spite of the great power of your spells...and destruction about which you do not know will come on you suddenly." Isa. 47:5-11 NAS.

God's judgment upon historical Babylon foreshadows His judgment upon spiritual Babylon. When we go to Babylon, we are more than captives in Babylon. We run the risk of becoming Babylonians. If we stay in Babylon and in our idolatries, we can expect God's judgment to fall upon us. We can expect a time when God will empty the Babylonian systems of His children, leaving them childless and without husbands. Isaiah 47, quoted above, has as much to do with God's impending judgment upon us in spiritual Babylon as it did upon historical Babylon.

Revelation predicts that a time is coming when an angel will come down out of heaven, having great authority, and will shout with a mighty voice, saying, "Babylon the great is fallen, is fallen, and has become the habitation of devils, and the hold of every foul spirit, and a cage of every unclean and hateful bird. For all nations have drunk of the wine of the wrath of her fornication, and the kings of the earth have committed fornication with her, and the merchants of the earth are waxed rich through the abundance of her delicacies." Rev. 18:2-3.

Then another voice from heaven was heard saying, "Come out of her, My people, that you might not be partakers of her sins, and that you not receive of her plagues." Rev. 18:4. This speaks of the one in Revelation 17:5 who had written upon her forehead the name,

"MYSTERY, BABYLON THE GREAT, THE MOTHER OF HARLOTS AND ABOMINATIONS OF THE EARTH."

Coming out of spiritual Babylon is not easy. We are comfortable there. The institutionalized *church* makes us feel safe, secure, and sufficient. *It* gives us status, position, reputation, security, and identity. We have become institutionalized within the institutions of our own making.

Chapter 7

Institutionalized

Bob and Joy, Chris and Jena, Troy, Rachel, and Darlene felt connected to one another in the Spirit of Christ and began meeting in each other's homes. They sang spiritual songs, shared revelations and teachings the Lord gave them. Bob did most of the teaching. He had the gift for it. They prayed for each other's needs. People were free to come and go as they pleased. When word got out that God was showing up at their meetings, more people started coming. They soon outgrew their living rooms and decided to rent a meeting room elsewhere. They took up a collection for the expenses. The crowd grew and they decided Bob needed to go full time as their pastor. The money was plentiful and in order to act responsibly, they decided to open a bank account. The bank required a name. So they named themselves. They continued to grow and decided to save rent expenses by buying their own piece of property. They elected elders to oversee the business they were growing into. Several years later, they occupied their fine new building for which they were indebted. But something different had happened. People no longer felt as free to come and go as they pleased. They were expected to be there and expected to pay their tithes there. They had a budget now. They went from being a fellowship of believers to a *church*. The day they gave themselves a name, they became a Thing. They institutionalized themselves.

Institutions seem to take on existences of their own as if they had minds of their own. They often become greater than the sum of the individuals who instituted them. They can take over and consume everything and everyone around them.

Yet, these institutions are devoid of life. They mesmerize, neutralize, ensnare, and enslave us. We become enmeshed with them and they become our idols. It is not long before our altruistic institutions—orphanages, nursing homes, colleges, universities, seminaries, hospitals, cemeteries, *church* edifices, and "ministries"—become more important than the people for whom they were initiated. People exist to serve and preserve them rather than them existing to serve the people. Their marketing programs may claim that they are meeting personal needs, and they may even be meeting personal needs, but the underlying motivation of their marketing schemes is often to increase their customer base in order to maintain or increase the institution.

Don Potter wrote in the Morning Star Journal that he had spoken to Jim Bakker after his release from prison, and Bakker admitted that he had questioned if God was in some of the things they were doing in his mega TV ministry. Things were growing so fast that no one would let him stop. Bakker couldn't imagine letting all those people down. Don commented, "He was caught in a ministry machine that had started running itself."[12] This happens to *churches* and ministries of all sizes.

Institutions often garner large sums of money from the people associated with them. People feel good about giving to them, but oftentimes come to realize that most of their time, energy, and resources are consumed merely to fuel the system. Altruism within the system is too frequently reduced to a token. Many TV ministries use altruistic appeals to tug on the emotions of potential donors, but end up using most of the money to keep their own ministry machine cranking.

INSTITUTIONALIZED

It is strange enough that these institutions seem to take on an existence of their own. It is stranger yet how our institutions institutionalize us.

Brooks "done time" in Shawshank prison for fifty years. He spent many of those years as the prison's librarian. Then it happened. He was paroled. Good news? Not for Brooks. He went crazy. They released him, and days later he was found hanging from a noose of his own making. The newer inmates didn't understand. They sat around on a rock waiting for Red to explain. Red had already spent most of his life behind those walls himself. He knew the score. Red answered philosophically. "He was institutionalized. Been in here fifty years. This is all he knows. In here, he's an important man. He's an educated man. But outside he's nothing. Just a used-up con with arthritis in both hands. Probably couldn't get a library card if he tried...These walls are funny. At first you hate 'em. Then you get used to them. Enough time passes, you get so you depend on them. That's institutionalized."[13]

[13]Don Potter, "Talent For Sale," *The Morning Star Journal* (Charlotte, NC: Morning Star Publications, Summer 1997) Vol. 7, No. 3, 63.

[13]*The Shawshank Redemption*, produced by Nike Marvin, directed by Frank Darnbont. Based on a novel by Steven King, titled, *Rita Hayworth and the Shawshank Redemption*.

BECOMING LIKE THEM

The longer we stay in our institutions, the more we become like them. A few years ago I awakened from a dream in which someone said to me, "Be careful you don't become like the club you join." This saying had a twist of humor to it when I heard it in the dream. On the one hand, it sounded like a warning not to become what I join. On the other hand, it was suggesting I already was like the club I joined. Why else would I join it? A club is made up of people. Once you join the club, you are the club. Once you join a *church,* you are that *church.*

Something in us draws us to the things we join. Soon after we join those things, they seem to have a way of possessing us. They become us and we become them. We find our identity in them. We boast, "I am Presbyterian." "I am Southern Baptist." "I am Methodist." "I am Roman Catholic." "I am Pentecostal." Then, we cannot resist asking others, "What are you?"

Jesus told us that we were in Him and He was in us, just as He was in the Father and the Father was in Him. That was not my experience growing up in the institutional *church.* I felt more joined to *it* than to Christ. I was in *it* and *it* was in me. I was programmed to be one with *it* and to bring others into that illegal, unholy, mystical union with *it.* We are either in Christ or in the harlot.

BELIEVING WHAT THEY BELIEVE

To truly belong to one of these institutions, we are somewhat required to believe what we are told to believe by those who rule within them. We often do not know what we believe ourselves apart from the doctrines of our *church.* Jerry Wilson recounts, "While studying for the ministry a fellow student began asking me questions about what I believed. I answered each one by telling him what the Baptists believe. I continued on for a while. Then he smiled and asked, 'Don't *you* believe anything?'"

We are to believe in Jesus. Our faith in God through Jesus Christ is how we are brought into the Kingdom. "For by grace are you saved through faith; and that not of yourselves; it is the gift of God." Eph. 2:8. Believing what our institution says to believe will not save us. Yet, we tend to think it does.

BECOMING DEPENDENT UPON THEM

Just as Brooks became dependent upon those walls at Shawshank prison, so we become dependent upon our institutions. We trust in them to take care of us. In a similar way, our institutions need us. The authorities within them need for us to be dependent upon them and the institution in order to perpetuate their existence and that of the institution.

Bill Shipman noticed this dependency principle when he worked at a developmental center for young offenders. Rather than encouraging them to become productive citizens, the authorities did things that made the inmates more dependent. If one of the inmates showed any individuality, they were prescribed more Valium. Those in charge wanted to conform them rather than reform them because they needed the inmates to be dependent upon them.

On several occasions Bill tried to get some of the inmates out of institutional dependency but was undercut by other staff members. They used fear to keep their young men feeling inadequate about themselves. "You better not listen to Bill," they would say. "You'll get out there and it'll just be a matter of time before you're back in here again."

"I saw things in this institution," Bill related, "that looked just like what I'd seen in the *church* by heavy-handed leaders with selfish ambition. It's okay when you're bettering the institution or bettering their positions, but when you try to better the clients—the people in need—you're booed down."

"This same thing happened in Haiti," Bill remembered. "The priests first came to Haiti with a mission to truly help the people. Under the influence of the government, the politically-minded superiors in the *church* persuaded the priests to do otherwise. They were told to teach the slaves that they were second-class citizens in the Kingdom of God and the only way that they could get in the Kingdom was by serving the whites. The black Haitians came to believe that about themselves. It is still difficult for them to break out of that thinking. That idea is institutionalized in their thinking."

You cannot preserve the institution and, at the same time, work to put yourself out of business. Institutions may start out to do good, but by their very nature, almost always end up fostering dependency.

PREEMINENCE OF THE INSTITUTION

Our institutions often become more important than the people for whom they were intended. Here is a case in point. The year was 1750. Jesuit missions were located around the border lands of Argentina, Paraguay, and Brazil. The Portuguese wanted to take possession of that territory and required the mission to transfer their territory to them. War was waged against the mission and many of the natives lost their lives in the ensuing battle. In the movie *The Mission*, about this true story, Father Gabriel was puzzled by the decision of his superiors to sacrifice the lives of the natives in order to comply with the Portuguese demands.

Señor Hatar, trying to make Father Gabriel understand, asked what he thought was at issue here.

"I think the work of God is at issue here," Father Gabriel naively answered.

"No," answered Señor Hatar. "What is at issue here is the very existence of the Jesuit order both here and in Europe."

To save the order, Señor Hatar did what he thought he had to do. He allowed the slaughter of many natives and the destruction of the mission. His rationale: "If the Jesuits resist the Portuguese, then the Jesuit order will be expelled from Portugal—and if Portugal and Spain, perhaps Italy, who knows. If your [Jesuit] order is to survive at all, Father, the mission here must be sacrificed."[14] The preservation of the institution—in this case the Jesuit order—was a greater cause than the lives of the people they came to save.

When we see the truth and attempt to speak against the abuses of institutionalization, we are viewed as the enemy. We are of no use to the institution. When we cease to be of use to the institution, the institution seeks ways to expel us.

THE CORPORATION *CHURCH*

Many *church* organizations have chosen to incorporate themselves according the laws of the states, primarily to receive tax breaks and to offer tax deductions for donors. *Churches* are ordinarily have this tax status without having to legally incorporate. Nevertheless, whether they have officially incorporated or not, most have structured themselves according to the principles and policies of corporations. They turn who they are as a fellowship of believers into a business and give this business the power to control the activities of their members.

The corporation *church,* like corporations in the world, have distinct characteristics. They are typically human-initiated and governed, management-based, profit-oriented, success-driven, client-friendly, product-focused (programs and services), and image-conscious.

A distinction must be made between the corporations of men from the body of Christ. We are not necessarily serving God and contributing to His causes just because we serve and contribute to these corporations. The ministry of Christ is accomplished in and

---

[14]*The Mission,* produced by Fernando Ghia, David Puttman, and Iain Smith (associate), directed by Roland Jaffe, writing credits to Robert Bolts. Distributed by Warner Brothers, 1986.

through the members of the body of Christ as they serve each other, not through legal documents in filing cabinets. God's building is not made with hands, but is eternal in the heavens. 2 Cor. 5:1.

This corporation *church* mentality is a modern invention of the western world which is completely foreign to the New Testament expression of what it means to be the body of Christ. Yet, missionary boards and Christian zealots peddle the principles and policies of the corporation *church* mentality around the world. This worldly concept is promoted as the only way to do *church*. Believers who dare to stand outside of this system are thought to have backslidden. Bob Hughey says, "What began as a movement in Israel became a philosophy in Greece, became an institution in Rome, became a culture in Europe, and became a big rich enterprise in America."

INSTITUTIONAL HIERARCHIES

All institutions whether governmental, educational, social, scientific, or religious have some form of hierarchical power-positions structured into them. These are the old guard, so to speak, those who not only have vested authority but exercise strict control. Very little, if anything, is allowed to happen without their say-so. It is no less true in the *churches*.

This hierarchy is often tiered as in the Roman Catholic, Anglican, or Eastern Orthodox traditions. The highest position within the Roman *church* is the Pope who is given extraordinary authority and esteem. The college of Cardinals are tiered under the Pope, having been appointed by the Pope to assist him. Bishops in the Roman Catholic, Anglican, or Eastern Orthodox traditions are clergymen who rank above a priest and have authority to ordain and confirm, and usually govern a diocese. In these traditions, Priests are clergymen who rank below a bishop and are authorized to perform the sacred rites of their *churches*. Deacons in these traditions are clerics who rank next below a priest. In most other traditions of Christian *churches*, deacons are laymen who are elected to perform various functions in worship, pastoral care, or administration.

Less liturgical traditions, such as we have in most Protestant *churches*, have their own form of hierarchy. Nearly all *church* groups have some form of high court in their general assemblies, conventions, or conferences to which officers are elected and given limited powers. People rarely stay in office long enough to build a political machine.

However, control in these traditions is more likely to come

through certain individuals of influence who are sometimes hidden within the system. Hugh was one of those men. He quietly influenced much of his denomination's social policies. For more than four decades from his hired, bureaucratic position at his denomination's headquarters, he remolded the theology of this *church* from conservative to liberal.

Some associations have been formed to cluster independent *churches* of like nature. These associations are generally headed by a charismatic personality who in turn has an inner circle of drones to help fulfill his agenda—a variation on the Pope and Cardinal scenario. Local assemblies, likewise, have positions of hierarchical authority within them—pastors, elders, deacons, and boards. Many Pentecostal traditions have bishops who are given greater esteem than others. These hierarchies within the *churches* are the traditions of men and have no basis in scripture, but appear necessary for the perpetuation of institutions.

INSTITUTIONAL RULES AND REGULATIONS

Many things have been started in the Spirit and founded upon solid scriptural principles, but were later institutionalized. The process is quite simple, natural, and common. Once the activity has begun, men tend to want to organize it. They wish to put some kind of structure around it in order to control it or at least maintain control within it. Institutional structure is generally made of rigid rules and regulations. Once set in place, these rules are hard to change. They become the authority over even those who made them. Even the people who make them bind themselves to the rules and, thereby, elevate the rules as the higher authority.

Organization requires rules. Once we *institute* rules and regulations to govern our relationships with one another, we have almost always *institutionalized* ourselves. We restrict the Holy Spirit's liberty to lead us. Control is one of the greatest enemies to our liberty in the Spirit. The rules men make to control *church* life are likely to become unhealthy boundaries. We often become slaves to these rules.

Nevertheless, good rules provide healthy boundaries and are necessary even for our participation in one another's lives in the body of Christ. These rules are generally in the category of "love one another." The word of God is the law of God and serves the well-being of those who keep it. We have the ability to keep God's law by the power of the Holy Spirit at work within us.

All too often, however, the rules of the institution supersede the word and Spirit of God. Such was the case when I believed the Holy

Spirit wanted to abolish the Sunday School. The rules of the organization did not allow that. "We don't do that here" is the common excuse. *Church* rules confine the activities of the Holy Spirit.

We need to distinguish between God's law which sets us free in Christ and *church* laws which impose restrictions upon us and bind us to men.

The institution of *church* is one among many of our Babylonian inventions and is perpetuated by those in THE Ministry.

Chapter 8

THE Ministry

*W*hile driving home one drizzling winter day after sharing with some believers in Georgia, I kept hearing the words rumbling around inside of me: "Quit the Ministry." That word was most troubling because I thought I had already done that. Still, there it was, relentlessly hounding me: "Quit the Ministry." Then I noticed the emphasis on the article: "Quit THE Ministry." I knew it was a refining word of God at work within me. THE Ministry, with the emphasis on the article "THE" and a capital "M," was a stronghold inside of me that had been passed down to me through the generations of religious tradition. This stronghold is what we call being in THE Ministry.

"What does it mean to quit THE Ministry?" I asked my wife, Nancy. As usual, with keen perception, knowing it had to do with me in particular, she thoughtfully answered. "It means not feeling responsible for the people in the little groups we minister to, making a syllabus or a book of everything that comes to you, systematizing everything into a formal teaching with the idea you have to teach it, starting a ministry school, putting out newsletters, nor pastoring anyone. It means to just *be*."

"I understand that," I told her, "but I don't know how to quit. How do I quit what has been programmed into me since childhood?"

From that beginning, the Holy Spirit opened my eyes to see some things about THE Ministry and began to set me free from the false expectations that go with being in THE Ministry.

IDOLATROUS EXTENSION OF SELF

On the outside, THE Ministry appears to be a noble life devoted to the sacrifice of Self; but when the inside is exposed, it is found to be a life of self-centeredness and self-exaltation. Just as it is with that Thing we call *church*, so is it with THE Ministry. It, too, is an idolatrous extension of Self, a Thing that exists outside of and in addition to the one in ministry. It is a mantle we put on ourselves that God has not woven for us.

We make a Thing out of being in ministry when we surmise, "I am *in* ministry, therefore, I *have* a ministry." Many well-meaning saints have started Ministries on the basis of an unusual testimony or an unusual gifting. It is good to have a testimony. It is good to share our testimonies. That is probably why we have them, but we do not have to go into THE Ministry just because we have a testimony. We do not have to go into THE Ministry just because we have a gifting to evangelize, prophesy, heal, teach, sing, or even preach. We do not have to go into THE Ministry just because we feel God's call to serve. God has called us all to minister. We are to do the ministry of the saints.

Paul, the apostle, illustrated how we are all members of the body of Christ and each has a different function. These functions are gifts and services to one another in the body. Paul said that if we have the gift of prophecy, then we are to prophesy according to the proportion of our faith. If we have the gift to ministry, then we are to minister. If teaching, then teach. If exhortation, then exhort. If giving, then give with simplicity. If ruling, then do it with diligence, If you show mercy, then do it with cheerfulness. Rom. 12:6-8. Nowhere does he remotely suggest that we are to get a private, non-profit corporation, name it, and solicit funds for it so we can be who we are in the body of Christ. Just do according to who you are.

When we start out in THE Ministry, we start something God has not started because we are wanting something for Self. We get possessive of this thing we call Ministry. We refer to it as "MY Ministry," or "THIS Ministry." We even make a business out of it. We name it, incorporate it, build a database for it, solicit funds for it, and traffic our giftings like five-and-dime store merchandise.

OBLIGATIONS OF THE MINISTRY

When one chooses to enter THE Ministry as a career, profession, or mind-set, he needlessly adopts a system of false obligations he feels inside of himself that enslaves him to that Thing we call THE Ministry. Here are some of those false obligations:

The one in THE Ministry feels obligated to think of himself, behave himself, and perform his duties in a certain way in order to live up to the expectations that go with his *ministerial* position. He feels obligated to produce sermons, perform rituals, conduct services, visit parishioners, develop programs, print bulletins, mail out newsletters, increase numerical growth, boost the finances, write books, sell tapes, be on television and radio, dress the code, and in some circles heal the sick and work miracles. These are the kinds of things that falsely attest to his success.

The one in THE Ministry feels obligated to set up the playground in which we can play *church*, so that he can lead the rest of us in playing *church*. Playing *church* is doing anything religious that is not inspired and empowered by the Holy Spirit. It is faithfully doing all of those things we do at *church* that make us feel like we have done our religious duty. We play *church* by the way we dress up to go there, by the pretentious ways we greet each other, by the programs and rituals we follow, by the way we line up in pews, and by the way we do things *at* each other without ever having a sense of involvement *with* each other. We more accurately express what it means to *be* the body of Christ when we do things *with* and *for* one another. Our gathering together should be "to consider one another to provoke unto love and to good works...exhorting one another: and so much the more, as you see the day approaching." Heb. 10:24-25. We accomplish these things by being sensitive to the Holy Spirit who alone knows how to minister to our individual needs. We minister to one another by the Spirit with the gifts of the Spirit named in 1 Corinthians 12:1-11.

The one in THE Ministry feels obligated to justify his ministry. He relies upon phony outward proofs of his success by counting noses, increasing the budget, multiplying his salary, building bigger buildings, making more visitations, keeping longer hours in the office, counseling more people, increasing the number of programs, acquiring more invitations to minister, scheduling more TV appearances, engaging a wider listening audience, and selling more books and tapes. Could this be the driving force for those who post the attendance and offering records on the *church* wall each Sunday with a comparison to "this time last year?"

The one in THE Ministry feels obligated to present himself in a certain way to his public that will impress them so they will approve of him. It may be in the way he dresses, the way he grooms his hair, or the way he talks; it may be in the kind of car he drives and house he lives in.

The one in THE Ministry feels obligated to be pious and religious, pretending to be more spiritual than he truly is. He becomes hypocritical as he puts on his phony religious mask. Piety and religion have nothing to do with the simplicity of following Jesus in honesty and brokenness and allowing His Holy Spirit to change us from the inside out.

The one in THE Ministry feels obligated to stay somewhat aloof from other saints. As a result, those in THE Ministry often form exclusive fraternities as evidenced in the existence of ministerial associations, the holding of clergy conferences, and other gatherings that bolster the unscriptural existence of clergy and laity.

The one in THE Ministry today more frequently feels obligated to establish a legal corporation to provide tax exemptions for their contributors. Often, however, this paper entity becomes more than a tax provision. It becomes the name and image of "his" ministry. He presents himself as the president and founder of it. He speaks of "this Ministry" in the third person as though it was the source from which the ministry of Christ flows. In so doing, he makes himself appear bigger than God has made him to be.

The one in THE Ministry feels obligated to start something—anything. He cannot present himself as idle. He organizes, institutionalizes, formalizes, establishes, and systematizes things. He, with deep heartfelt concerns, starts things in his own strength and has to keep those things going in his own strength. When he stops working his plan, his plans stop working for him. But what God starts in Holy Spirit power, God finishes in Holy Spirit power.

The one in THE Ministry feels obligated to build his reputation and to market his talents, gifts, and wares. Consequently, he has to have his own public relations program to promote himself. He proudly puts his name and his face on the work that he believes God has called him to do. Whereas James wrote, "God resists the proud, but gives grace to the humble...Humble yourselves in the sight of the Lord, and He shall lift you up." James 4:6,10.

The one in THE Ministry feels obligated to know more about the Bible and religion than those he ministers to. Thus, he is obligated to achieve academic prowess which often opens him up to pride and intellectualism. He is not content for people to just know. He has a need for people to know that *he* knows. He feels obligated to compete with other ministers to know as much or more as they and to be as good or better than they. He sometimes feels it is necessary to keep those he ministers to ignorant; thus dependent upon him.

The one in THE Ministry feels obligated to solicit support for his ministry whether from his "partners" or from a salaried position. When he receives a salary for his so-called leadership role in the body of Christ, he makes a distinction between himself and the sheep. He ignores the fact that he, too, is a sheep and that all sheep are in ministry. The one in THE Ministry lacks faith in God's ability to use him in season and provide for him without having to manipulate others into supporting "his" ministry.

The one in THE Ministry feels obligated to have a title for himself—Pastor, Reverend, Bishop, Apostle, Doctor. The more prestigious the title, the better. Bob Hughey says, "Titles divide; function unifies. A testimony is more important than a title."

The one in THE Ministry feels obligated to clone others to be like him or his kind of *church*. He needs to clone them in order to own them. If he does not own them, he fears losing their support.

The one in THE Ministry feels obligated to be set apart from the "laity" by being ordained. Many *church* traditions ordain their clergy through what the historical *church* calls "apostolic succession." Apostolic succession is the perpetuation of spiritual authority by the successive ordination of clergy from the time of the apostles. One must be ordained in apostolic succession in the Roman Catholic, Anglican, and Eastern Orthodox traditions in order to administer the sacraments and orders. While Barnabus and Paul were confirmed as apostles by the prophets and teachers in Antioch (Acts 13:1-3) and elders were to be appointed in every city (Titus 1:5), the common tradition of ordination as it is practiced in western Christianity is not found in the New Testament. Barnabas and Paul were not set apart by the twelve apostles but by certain teachers and prophets in Antioch. Acts 13:1-3. The anointing for ministry comes from God and not from men. Eph. 4:11.

The one in THE Ministry feels obligated to perpetuate the industry of THE Ministry. THE Ministry is big business. It drives the economy of seminaries and Bible colleges, *churches* with their staff positions, new church construction, church furnishings, Ministries, publishing houses, recording companies, book stores, conferences, and radio and television shows. It is a web of economic support in which the Minister himself becomes entangled and from which he cannot easily break away. Those in THE Ministry live compromised lives under the influences of man-pleasing spirits. The merchants who peddle their wares to those in THE Ministry and those who are in THE Ministry are dependent upon each other for their existence. This mutual dependency for existence is another reason why this whole system is a stronghold not easily pulled down.

The one in THE Ministry feels obligated to perpetuate the institution of THE Ministry as well as the institution of *church*. THE *Ministry is an institution within the institution of church and is the singular most powerful force that perpetuates the institution of church.* If we were to remove this erroneous notion of THE Ministry from the equation of *church*, this Thing we call *church* would fall apart. Similarly, without the *church* system, THE Minister would have no context in which to practice his craft. *Church* is sustained by money. Once the money ends, the *church* institution folds. Likewise, when the money ends, THE Ministry ends because those in THE Ministry depend upon the money and the system.

THE DATABASE

The one in THE Ministry feels obligated to build a database in order to maintain visibility with his supposed supporters. He lives under the fearful code: "out of sight, out of mind." He may keep a record of the baptisms, weddings, and funerals he has performed, as well as the number of attendees to his meetings and new members he takes in as though they were notches in his spiritual gun handle.

He who owns a database for the purpose of increasing himself in ministry wants to broaden his sphere of influence.

He tends to think he owns the people on his database.

He tends to think that he has a responsibility toward the people listed on his database—that he needs to answer to them.

He tends to think the people on his database owe him support for "his ministry."

He tends to measure his success in THE Ministry by the size of his database. Names are like trophies. The more he has, the more he wants and the better he thinks he is. He may periodically, with pride, inventory the numbers just to see how many are on his mailing list.

He can become obligated to his database even if those names are no more than a short fax or e-mail list. The database can own a part of him and put him in bondage to it. He has not quit THE Ministry until he has trashed his self-serving databases. Inability to trash his self-serving database may indicate that it is an idol in his life.

The key word here for those in THE ministry is "self-serving." Most of the "newsletters" I have seen read like a brochure promoting the one in THE Ministry who sent it out, most of whom are seeking financial support for themselves.

We must honestly evaluate: Does our database exist to increase ourselves or Jesus? John the Baptist caught a glimpse of the Kingdom of God when he said, "He [Jesus] must increase, but I must decrease. John 3:30. THE Ministry is a ministry of the increase of Self, while true "ministry" is the ministry of the increase of Christ in others.

FULL-TIME PROFESSIONALS

The one in THE Ministry often seeks it as a full-time career or occupation in the hope that it might provide an income for him. Such was the case with John and Sue. Ellie wrote about them:

> It had been some time since I had heard from Sue. I was happy to hear from her but felt the same emotions I feel when friendly telemarketers call. Uncertain about my perception, I continued a friendly conversation. Both of our

families were free not to be a part of a local *church* and had independently decided to stay home on Sunday mornings. Since then, however, Sue and her husband, John, had started a *church* of their own.

Finally, she got around to asking where we were going to *church*. I told her we felt we were not to be in a *church* at this time. She sighed and made a comment about how much time they were spending in prayer. "When you start a work you need to spend a lot of time in prayer" she said. "In fact," she added, "we still don't really know if..." Her voice and vocabulary failed her. I could tell she was sad to think their work might not continue to provide them with a livelihood. In an attempt to encourage her I said, "No matter what happens, the growth you are seeing and the relationship you are developing with these other people is eternal and above *The Ministry* and *A Work.*"

Sue replied in all sincerity, "We really feel called to the ministry, and if the ministry is going to be our livelihood, then at some point it has to be viable and more than just a couple of families meeting in a living room."

Ministry in the Holy Spirit comes out of who we are in Jesus and is not a position to attain to in the world. When we need to have a congregation in order to provide an income for ourselves, we have a harlot condition in our hearts. We are seeking something for Self. If we are truly called to be elders who shepherd God's sheep, we are to feed His sheep. God forbid that we would seek to feed off them.

THE SEDAN CHAIR

"It was supposedly a time of celebration," Bill Shipman recalled. "We were sending some leaders from our church to Chicago to start a new church. We showered them with expensive gifts while ignoring the needs of others in our midst. One couple," he remembered, "needed a refrigerator. They were having to buy ice. It was an imbalance."

Bill, sharing a vision he had from the Holy Spirit about this, saw these men being lifted up on very ornate and gaudy sedan chairs.

The chairs were gilded and had curly swirls and fancy tapestries hanging down with tassels on the top. The sedan chairs looked heavy. These men were being lifted up and carried by the little ones in the church. The little ones were glad to try to carry them as they started out across a desert.

The Holy Spirit spoke a word of warning to those leaders being sent out saying, "You are going out, but you're going out on your own will. You're not going in My will."

Soon after they went out, I saw that those who were carrying the leaders became weak and the sedan chairs tottered. The people kept trying to hold them up financially, praying for them, interceding for them, but everyone kept getting more weary. Finally, out of exhaustion, everyone had to let go. The sedan chairs fell and broke up.

"These brothers and sisters in Chicago were having a hard time financially," Bill said. "They sold their homes before they left. They did not make the best use of God's resources the way it was done. It was done in self-centeredness. People began to leave. They could not hold them up any longer. The leadership felt abandoned, but it wasn't abandonment. The children should never have been made to carry the fathers; the fathers are made to carry the children."

FALSE FLOW CHARTS

"False leaders still want to dust off those sedan chairs and get the people under them," Bill observed. "This is happening around the world. The leaders of this Haitian mission proudly displayed their organizational flow chart. The name of the main leader in the mission was positioned at the top of the pyramid. Next in line were other leaders with the people forming the base line. They asked me, 'What do you think about this?'

"'Do you really want to know?' I asked in return.

"'Sure, Brother Bill.'

"If Jesus walked in right now, He'd rip it off the wall and turn it upside down, and say, 'Now, that's a flow chart.'"

Bill concluded. "True leaders put the people in the place of honor and carry them in sedan chairs that are graced with tender care and mercy. If the minister does not see himself as one among the bride of Christ, he will rape the bride by using her to increase himself."

The Babylonian Minister views himself as not only having been set *apart* but having been set *above* the "laity." He is the "professional." He takes on titles for himself in his personal ambition to build for himself a city, a tower, and a name. Reputation is very important to him. Though he calls himself their servant, more often than not the flock is called upon to serve him, his plans, and programs. Yet, he is forever busy doing the work of the *church* in the place of the people—*church* work, not kingdom of God work.

Tradition has obligated this one-man-show ministry to fulfill many functions that are not within his gifting. Many in THE Ministry enter into pride when they try to take on responsibilities that do not pertain to their giftings. Such pride and ambition often leads to frustration and burnout.

SERVANTS

Whether we say we are "*in* THE Ministry" or "*have* a Ministry," we assume something that is foreign to the idea of ministry in the New Testament. THE Ministry with the upper case "M" is a Babylonian concept whereas the idea of ministers with the lower case "m" is quite New Testament. We do not have "a" Ministry. We are all *the* ministry of Christ. THE Ministry, as it has come to be conceptualized, is a hindrance to true New Testament ministry, because it stifles the saints from fulfilling their ministries. THE Ministry is in direct opposition to true New Testament ministry.

The word "ministry" in the New Testament is translated from several Greek words. *Doulos* (slave) and *diakonos* (servant) are two of the terms that have been translated "minister." All saints are ministers/servants according to the pattern set forth in the New Testament. While there are some the Lord Jesus appoints to be apostles, prophets, evangelists, shepherds (elders), and teachers, they are given to the body to equip the other saints for the work of service (ministry). Eph. 4:11-12. Those equipping servants (apostles, prophets, evangelists, shepherds and teachers) are not clergy positions within the *church.* They are not offices. The term office is not a Greek New Testament word.[15] Servant appointments are functions within the body of Christ. Those who exalt themselves as apostles, prophets, evangelists, pastors, and teachers are spots in our love feasts and clouds without water. Jude 12.

Those who have the mantle of a true elder do not use their giftings to lord it over the saints. They see themselves as being equal

---

[15]The King James Version uses the word "office" in several passages, but is translated from various Greek words that mean different things. In Luke 1:8, in reference to Zacharias who was performing his Old Testament priesthood, the word "office" means "to serve as priest" and in Luke 1:9, it simply refers to the priesthood. In Romans 11:3, the word "office" has been derived from *diakonian* which means "service." This phrase literally translates, "I magnify my serving." In Romans 12:4, the word office comes from a Greek word that means "action." In 1 Timothy 3:1, no word exists at all in the Greek text where the word "office" has been implied. In 1 Timothy 3:10, again, the word is from the root word *diakonas* (service) and should not read, "Let them use the office of a deacon", but should read, "Let them minister (or serve)..." In 1 Timothy 3:13, the word used there, *bathmon*, speaks of a manner in which one walks with dignity, rank, and standing.

among the flock. Paul warned the elders from Ephesus when they were together with him at Miletus to "be on guard for yourselves and for all the flock, *among* whom the Holy Spirit has made you overseers to shepherd the called-out-ones of God which He purchased with His own blood." Acts 20:28. Elders are *among* the sheep and not positioned piously *over* the sheep.

Paul warned them to keep watch over their own hearts because, after his departure, he knew that savage wolves would enter in among them, attacking the flock. Some among them would gain prominence, distort the truth, and draw away disciples to follow them. Acts. 20:29-30. Ministers of *churches* today are just as territorial. They chase off anyone they perceive might steal "their" sheep. They seem to forget that the saints of God are not their sheep! They are His sheep!

The servant does not seek to exalt himself—to increase himself in power, position, riches, and domination. He is content to remain nameless and faceless in order to serve when, where, and how the Holy Spirit leads. He does this without expecting anything for Self.

FOLLOWING JESUS

I called Bill Shipman to tell him I had quit THE Ministry. After pondering my announcement for a moment, he answered with glee in his voice, "I thought we were just supposed to follow Jesus."

Quitting THE Ministry does not mean inactivity. We have a walk to walk. We are to follow Jesus wherever He goes, and we do not have to turn it into a business, put a name on it, or put a title on ourselves.

Each of us has a gifting—a ministry—with a little 'm,' whether large or small, that we are responsible to steward. We have a responsibility to respond to the Holy Spirit when He prompts us to operate in that gift or ministry for the edification of the body, that we might build one another up into a spiritual dwelling as the household of God. Eph. 2:19-22. These are functions and not positions.

THE Ministry implies that some among us are big shots and the rest of us are inconsequential. It implies a one-up, one-down relationship between those who are especially gifted from all the rest of us. If ever there were big shots in the Kingdom of God, the chosen twelve apostles would certainly qualify. Nevertheless, Jesus told His twelve that they were not to be like the princes of the Gentiles who lorded their authority over the people. Matt. 20:25-26. With the twelve then, and even so for us today, "whoever will be great among you, let him be your minister [*diakonos* which literally translates "servant"] and whoever will be chief among you, let him be your servant [*doulos* which literally translates "slave"]; even as the Son of man came not to be ministered unto, but to minister [*diokonesai* which literally translates "to serve"], and to give His life a ransom for many." Matt. 20:27-28.

The five equipping servants of Ephesians 4:8 have the anointings to equip the rest of the body of Christ for the work of service, but this does not make them greater than the rest of the body of Christ. Those with the apostolic anointing are at best under-rowers. Recounting his conversion experience before Agrippa, Paul quoted the Lord as having said to him, "But arise, and stand upon your feet for I have appeared to you for this purpose, to make you a *minister*." Acts 26:16. The word for minister used here comes from the root *huperetes* which literally means "under-rower." This nautical term generally denotes any subordinate who works under the direction of another. Apostles are subservient to the authority of Christ who sets them apart and sends them out. In 1 Corinthians 3:21-4:1 Paul includes Apollos and Cephas as under-rowers: "Let a man so account of us, as of the *ministers* of Christ." This term was also used in reference to John Mark in Act 13:5.

I find that when I try to *do* ministry—that is, when I try to make it happen in my own strength, the anointing evades me. When I rest in being who I am without trying to *do* ministry, the anointing compels me. I am far more productive for the Kingdom when I maintain resignation from THE Ministry than when I actively pursue it. When I pursue THE Ministry, I miss the Kingdom. When I pursue the Kingdom, ministry (not THE Ministry) pursues me. True ministry is the measure of Jesus that He desires to pour out through me.

Many individuals who are in this Thing we call THE Ministry are Nicolaitans and have a Nicolaitan spirit.

Chapter 9

The Nicolaitans

Nicolaitans? Who were the Nicolaitans? They are mentioned only twice in the scriptures and both times with contempt. The first mention of them is in Revelation 2:6. The glorified Jesus told the old apostle John to write to the angel (messenger) of the called-out-ones in Ephesus. In this letter, Jesus praised the Ephesians for their works, labor, patience, and for the fact that they could not bear those who were evil. They had, furthermore, tested those who said they were apostles but were not, and had found them to be liars. The Lord severely admonished them, however, for having left their first love. Perhaps they had all the right doctrines and were doing the good works of a Christian, but were showing more affection for the *things* of the gospel than for the *person* of the gospel. Whatever the Ephesians were doing that caused them to leave their first love, it was severe enough for the Lord to call them to repentance. If they did not repent, He would remove their candlestick from them. He would remove the power, presence, and the light of His Holy Spirit. Then the Lord praised them saying, "But this you have, that you hate the deeds of the Nicolaitans, which I also hate."

The only other reference to the Nicolaitans is in Revelation 2:15. The called-out-ones in Pergamos had those among them who held to the doctrine (teachings) of the Nicolaitans. Regarding them Jesus said, "So you also have those who hold the doctrine of the Nicolaitans, which thing I hate." He hated what they were teaching.

From these two references, we know that the Lord hated their "deeds" and their "doctrines" (teachings). It appears that we are left to speculate about who they were, what their deeds were, and what they taught. Not so! The evidence of what they did and what they taught is revealed in scripture. We learn who they were by what they did and what they taught. By this, we learn who they are in the *churches* today.

NICOLAITANS' NAME

The first clue as to who they were can be found in what they were called—Nicolaitans. The word Nicolaitan comes from two Greek words: *nike* and *laios*. *Nike* means "to conquer," "subdue," "overcome," and *laos* refers to a body of people, the common people. *Nikos* is the equivalent to *nike* and has been translated "victory." When combined, these two terms translate "conqueror [or subduer] of the common people."

These "conquerors of the people" were among the assembly of called-out-ones in Ephesus and Pergamos. They obviously had some major influence among the saints.

(Some scholars say they were followers of Nicolas who was one of the deacons in Acts 6:5. They speculate that Nicolas went into deception and led some of the believers away from the faith. This is impossible to document.)

Their name represents who the Nicolaitans were and what they taught. They were those who positioned themselves above the "common" people as having some authority over them and taught that this was the way things were supposed to be. I believe this was the beginning of the clergy system that came into prominence in the historical, institutional *church* system.

The clergy refers to persons who are ordained for religious service such as ministers, priests, and rabbis. The word cleric is sometimes used in relation to a clergy person. Clericalism is the "political influence or power of the clergy, or a policy or principles favoring this: generally a derogatory term."[16] The clergy system in the *churches* advocates the elevation of the "professional" ministers above common believers.

ASSOCIATED WITH BALAAM

The second clue as to who the Nicolaitans were is found in the association of their name with Balaam. In Revelation 2:15, the King James Version translation reads, "So you *also* have those who hold to the doctrine of the Nicolaitans..." The word "also" comes from the Greek word *kai* which can be translated "and," "also," or "even" depending upon the context in which it is used. The Greek text has, in addition to *kai,* the word *omoios* which means "likewise." Some of the translations dropped *omoios* and missed an important aspect of interpretation. The New American Standard kept it and translated it, "in the same way." It reads, "Thus, you *also* have some who *in the same* way hold the teaching of the Nicolaitans."

We ask, "in the same way" as who? The answer to that question is found in the previous verses. In Revelation 2:14-15, the Lord said, "But I have a few things against you, because you have there those who hold the doctrine of Balaam, who taught Balak to cast a

---

[16]*Webster's New World Dictionary,* 2nd college ed., s.v. "clericalism."

stumbling block before the children of Israel, to eat things sacrificed to idols, and to commit fornication. Thus, you *also* have some who *in the same* way hold the teaching of the Nicolaitans." I suggest, therefore, that this reference to Balaam is the antecedent of the phrase "in the same way." "The doctrine of Balaam" (v. 14) and "the doctrine of the Nicolaitans" (v.15) is referring to the same thing or things.

If, therefore, "the doctrine of Balaam" is that to which the phrase "in the same way" refers, then it is necessary to find out more about Balaam in order to find out more about the Nicolaitans.

SAY, DO, AND BE

First, however, consider these three virtues of God's true ministers: they will *say* what God says, *do* what God says do, and *be* what God wants them to be. They cannot do otherwise. They are unlike Balaam in the Old Testament as told about in Numbers 22-24. Balaam could not be what he was not.

Balak was the King of the Moabites at the time the Israelites pitched their tents in the land of Moab. Balak was fearful of what the Israelites might do to his people because he saw that they had struck the Amorites and taken their cities. So he sent messengers to hire Balaam to come and speak a curse against these Israelites who had come out of Egypt. Balaam was a non-Israelite prophet.

Balaam was certainly enticed by the price they offered him, but warned Balak that he was bound to *say* the words that God put in His mouth. Balaam did just that. He spoke four prophecies favoring Israel, and one opposing Balak. Why then was Balaam looked upon with such disdain in both the Old and the New Testaments?

Remember, it takes all three virtues to be a true minister of God: *say* what God says to say, *do* what God says to do, and *be* what God would have one to be. Balaam fell miserably short when it came to this third virtue to *be*. Here is how we know.

THE MATTER AT PEOR

Later on in Numbers 31, we read where God told Moses to take vengeance on the Midianites for the sons of Israel. He had sent his captains and warriors from every tribe and the priests with the holy vessels and the trumpets of alarm. They killed every male and the kings of Midian. They burned the cities and took the spoil, but they captured the women and brought them back with them.

Moses and others went out to meet his returning army and saw what they had done. He was angry with the officers and asked them why they had spared the women. It would seem like the noble thing to do, would it not? Moses explained his anger in verse 16: "Behold, these caused the children of Israel, through the counsel of Balaam, to commit trespass against the LORD in the matter of Peor."

So, what happened at Peor and what did Balaam have to do with that? Apparently everything! We see in Numbers 25 that Israel played the harlot with the daughters of Moab: "They called the people to the sacrifices of their gods: and the people ate and bowed down to their gods. And Israel joined himself to Baal-peor: and the anger of the LORD was kindled against Israel." Num. 25:2-3. Remember, God had made it emphatically clear that the Israelites were not to mingle with the people of the land. Deut. 7:1-6.

No reference is made whatsoever to Balaam in Numbers 25, but Numbers 31:16 informs us that this "sin" at Peor was due to the counsel of Balaam. In Numbers 22-24 we read how Balak offered both money and prestige to Balaam to get him to pronounce a curse against the Israelites. Balaam was not about to miss his opportunity for fortune and prominence.

Balaam must have known about this ban that God had set forth as recorded in Deuteronomy 7 and used it to defeat the Israelites. He "taught Balak to cast a stumbling block before the children of Israel, to eat things sacrificed to idols, and to commit fornication." Rev. 2:13. In other words, Balaam counseled Balak to entice the Israelite sons and daughters to mix with the sons and daughters of Moab. This way, Balaam did not have to speak the curse, but he ensured that Israel would place themselves under a curse. Israel did just that. They played the harlot and brought the curse of a plague upon themselves that killed twenty-four thousand of their own. Num. 25:9.

Balaam collected his blood money and prepared to live lavishly among the kings of Midian. His life, however, was short-lived after that. Numbers 31:8 tells us that he was killed with the sword when Israel took vengeance on the Midianites. He was a false prophet. He was bound to *say* what God wanted him to say. He was forced even by his jackass (donkey) to *do* what God wanted, but it was not in him to *be* what God would have him to be. He was greedy and sought to increase himself in power, position, riches, and domination. He put Himself above the concerns of God and God's people. We are much like Balaam when we ask God to bless our flesh rather than denying our flesh to obey God.

BALAAM'S NAME AND REPUTATION

Another connection between Balaam and the Nicolaitans is embedded in his name. Balaam's name is the combination of two words from the Hebrew: *beli* and *haam*. *Beli* means "conqueror" and, *haam* means "the people." Put them together and we get "conqueror of the people." Balaam's name, therefore, translates the same as Nicolaitan. Is this not strong evidence that the reference to Balaam is the antecedent of the phrase "in the same way"?

Balaam is also mentioned in 2 Peter 2:15 in the context of false teachers. The false teachers were those "who have forsaken the right way, and have gone astray, following the way of Balaam the son of Beor, who loved the wages of unrighteousness; but was rebuked for his iniquity; the dumb ass speaking with man's voice forbade the madness of the prophet."

He is mentioned with disdain in Jude, verse 11: "Woe to them," Jude writes, "for they...ran greedily after the error of Balaam for reward. " These three New Testament witnesses against Balaam are harsh to say the least. Each of them speak of greed. Nicolaitans cause God's people to commit spiritual fornication by joining them to their idolatrous *church* systems.

SELF-AGGRANDIZEMENT

Having looked into who Balaam was, we come back to our original question: Who, then, were the Nicolaitans? They were leaders within the Christian community who were false prophets "in the same way" as was Balaam. They were ministers among the assembly of called-out-ones who were motivated by greed and self-aggrandizement—the need to increase themselves in power, position, riches, and domination. They had managed to exalt themselves in leadership roles above those "common" called-out-ones.

The New Testament mentions Diotrephes, who possessed this Nicolaitan spirit. The end of the first century A.D. was nearing when the aged apostle John wrote his third epistle. He wrote to the well beloved Gaius and addressed his grief over one who was known as Diotrephes. It appears from the letter that Diotrephes had positioned himself in an uncommon place of authority among an assembly of called-out-ones. He loved to have preeminence among them. 3 John 1:9. He not only refused to welcome the apostle John and others of the brethren, but removed from the assembly those who did dare to welcome them. 3 John 1:10-11.

The desire for preeminence is a characteristic of the Nicolaitan spirit. Nicolaitans are those who seek to elevate themselves above the so-called laity. I say they are "so-called" because no such distinctions are made in the New Testament between professional clergy and laity. Such distinctions smack insults at the doctrine of the priesthood of all believers. The clerical exercise of such authority over the called-out-ones sprang up throughout all Christendom soon after the turn of the first century. This reference to Diotrephes in 3 John is clear evidence that it had already taken root. Nicolaitans are like goats. They like high places.

THE NICOLAITAN IN ME

I was raised in institutional Christianity. The Nicolaitan (clergy) spirit was programmed into me from childhood by those who had it programmed into them. It's generational. It was all I had ever seen or known. I had no way of knowing that ministry could be anything other than what my experiences and education taught me. So, I pursued the normal course of ministry that was expected of me.

I answered the call to ministry when I was about twelve years of age and enrolled immediately out of high school in the denominational college that trained me for ministry. Years later I finished with a Masters of Divinity degree from seminary.

I had taken the usual run of classes in Bible and religion that trained me to perpetuate the system I was in. I had been trained by the clergy system to be one of their own. I was hired by the elders of a local *church* to be their pastor. I was the chief administrator and, for all practical purposes, was the professional hired to lead the work of the *church*.

After twelve years behind the pulpit, I turned away from God and left the ministry. Following my conversion years later, God pinned me down in what I call my wilderness experience. It lasted for many years. God put me through His school of the Holy Spirit. This was a time of learning the word of God for myself, of receiving revelations, and of being purged of many spots and wrinkles.

One particular day on my wilderness journey, I was in prayer with the Lord when I saw in my mind's eye a miniature image of a man standing upon a high cliff, arms folded, chest puffed out, head cocked back, full of arrogance and pride. After doing a double-take, I said, "Lord, that looks like me!"

I knew that I was seeing a "spirit" of preeminence. I knew that it was the Nicolaitan spirit that had been implanted in me since early childhood. This was that clergy spirit of self-aggrandizement. As soon as I saw this, I renounced it and asked the Lord to separate it from me. It has taken years for that to happen.

THE RISE OF BISHOPS

This Nicolaitan spirit is deceptive and deadly. It is deeply entrenched in most of the men and women who have been trained and nurtured to minister in the *church* system. Nicolaitan personalities have ruled in the *churches* since the first century A.D.

In spite of those exceptions like Diotrephes, simplicity seemed to have characterized the life of the called-out-ones that we know about from the New Testament until after the death of John. Little is known about the activities of the called-out-ones for those few years between the death of John and the turn of the century.

When the pages of *church* history began to flip again into the beginning of the second century, an interesting thing had occurred. Certain ones bore the title of bishop, such as Polycarp of Smyrna, Clement of Rome, Ignatius of Antioch, Polybius of Tralles, and Onesimus of Ephesus. These were godly men, defenders of the faith, some of whom were martyrs for Jesus, but were nonetheless caught up in the power and position of the bishopric.

Justo Gonzalez points out in his *Story of Christianity* that James, the brother of Jesus, was erroneously given the title of "bishop" of Jerusalem by *church* leaders in later years.[17] Gonzalez explains that "the emphasis on the authority of bishops and on apostolic succession was a part of the response of the church to the challenge of heresies in the late second and early third centuries. As the church became increasingly Gentile, the danger of heresies was greater, and this in turn led to a greater stress on episcopal [bishop] authority."[18]

By the time of the monastic movement in the late third and early fourth centuries, bishops lived in great cities and enjoyed great power and prestige. Moreover, the bishopric had become an office to be filled rather than a calling by God upon a man. The story is told of a man named Martin, born in 335 A.D., who lived the monastic life and was elected to the office of bishop of Tours by popular demand. Gonzalez wrote, "When the bishopric of Tours became vacant, the populace wanted to elect Martin to that position. The story goes that some of the bishops present at the election opposed such an idea, arguing that Martin was unusually dirty, dressed in rags, and disheveled, and that his election would damage the prestige of the office of bishop."[19] This story tells us that the bishopric of Tours had become a position or office to which men could be elected. What was once a calling of God upon individual men has since become an institution of men.

Many churches in the Presbyterian tradition have elected men, women, and young people as elders to fill a certain number of

---

[17] Justo L. González, *The Story of Christianity: Volume 1, The Early Church to the Dawn of the Reformation* (San Francisco: Harper and Row, 1984) 21.

[18] González, 97.

[19] González, 149.

positions for limited terms. Where is any of this in the Bible?

According to New Testament records, elders were appointed in every city and they existed in plurality. No man was given that responsibility alone. Elders were not called bishop nor pastor. They were elders who shepherded the flock of God among whom the Holy Spirit had made them overseers (which is the Greek word *episcopous,* also translated "bishop"). Acts 20:28 NKJV. The terms elder, shepherd, and overseer refer to the same person. Elder has to do with *who* they were. Shepherd has to do with *what* they did. Overseer has to do with *how* they did what they did. An elder is one who is called of God to perform a function in the body of Christ and was never intended to be a position, office, title, or institution in the Kingdom of God.

This unscriptural "office" of bishop was the seedbed in which the hierarchical system of clergymen took root and flourished in the eventual rise of the Roman Catholic Church. The power of the office of bishop was such that simony became an issue in the *church.* Simony is the buying and selling of ecclesiastical *(church)* positions. Similarly, nobles, kings, and emperors were known to have appointed and invested bishops and abbots in order to have political control of the *church.*

The veneration that is bestowed upon popes, cardinals, bishops, and priests has to be most revolting to the Holy Spirit of God; especially that the Pope, a man, should be called, Holy Father. The word cardinal when used as an adjective means "of foremost importance; paramount."[20]

Jesus exhorted His followers regarding this need for veneration: "But you are not to be called Rabbi: for one is your Master, Christ; and all you are brethren. And call no man your father upon the earth: for one is your Father, which is in heaven. Neither are you to be called masters: for one is your Master, Christ. But he who is greatest among you shall be your servant. And whosoever shall exalt himself shall be abased; and he who humbles himself shall be exalted." Matt. 23:8-12.

In spite of the Reformation and other spiritual awakenings, the influence of the clergy system abounds in every denomination and independent *church.* Any challenge to a person's exalted position as "Pastor" (or whatever title they go by) are fighting words to most.

Nevertheless, I boldly declare that the Nicolaitans today are all those who promote the clergy system, which separates the so-called "professional" ministry from the so-called laity. They are those who

---

[20]*American Heritage Dictionary,* s.v. "cardinal."

seek to increase themselves in power, position, riches, and domination and generally do so at the expense of the saints. This "clergy system" is the work of the harlot spirit in the *churches.*

EAT THE SHEEP

The Nicolaitans are those shepherds of Ezekiel 34 whom God prophesied against for feeding themselves when they should have fed the flock. They ate the fat and clothed themselves with wool, killed those who were fed, did not strengthen the diseased, did not heal those who were sick, did not bind up those who were broken, did not bring back those who had been driven away, did not seek those who were lost, and ruled over the ones they did have with force and with cruelty. Their flocks were scattered and became meat to all the beasts of the field.

The Lord was against those shepherds. He said He would require His flock at their hands and cause them to cease from feeding the flock. They would no longer be able to feed themselves off of the flock because He promised to deliver His sheep from their mouths. His sheep would no longer be meat for them. Ezek. 34:2-5,10.

Dennis Loewen notes, "Balaam did great damage by advising Balak to entice the Israelites through whoredoms to ultimately serve foreign gods. The modern-day Nicolaitans exact the same final effect when they wed the people of God to a foreign god—to another Jesus." Nicolaitans take advantage of the sheep to advance themselves. They eat the sheep to fatten themselves.

The time is coming, however, when God Himself will take these sheep from the false shepherds. He will search for His sheep and seek them out Himself. He will feed, tend, lead, and heal them Himself. Ezek. 34:11-16.

Present-day Nicolaitans have the same marks of the Pharisees who lived in Jesus' day.

Chapter 10

The Marks of the Pharisees

*M*inisters who are smitten with the need for preeminence, power, position, riches, and domination have embraced the false teachings of the Nicolaitans and are likely to perpetuate both the teachings and the deeds of the Nicolaitans. They have the same marks that characterized the Pharisees in Jesus' day.

In Matthew 23:33, Jesus called the Pharisees "serpents" and a "generation of vipers." The Greek word for "generation" also translates "offspring." Here, Jesus is calling the Pharisees snakes and the offspring of snakes. He continues in verse 33, "How can you escape the damnation of hell?" The Bible identifies Satan as a serpent. Gen. 3:1-5; Rev. 12:9; 20:2. The association between Satan and the Pharisees is without dispute. Why did Jesus call the Pharisees snakes? What objection did He have to them? After all, they were devoutly religious and zealous to keep the law.

The scathing litany of woes spoken by Jesus in Matthew 23 define some of what were the detestable marks of the Pharisees. Though the differences between some of these marks of the Pharisees are little, they are important distinctions to make—not so much to judge others, but to judge the Pharisee in us all.

ABUSIVE USE OF AUTHORITY

Jesus hated the way the Pharisees misused and abused authority. Jesus said to the multitude and to His disciples, "The scribes and the Pharisees *sit in Moses' seat*." Matt. 23:1-2. The Pharisees assumed the position of authority over people's lives. They considered themselves experts on the law. Therefore, they presumed to tell everyone else how to live.

The present-day Nicolaitan attitude is seen in that air of self-importance that wants to sit at the head of the table, to be elected to positions of authority, or to be hired to some prestigious office. Nicolaitans typically politic for higher positions of preeminence and authority within the *church* systems. They flatter themselves and seek the flattery of others. Moreover, they pass gavels of authority to designate someone among them as the head over them. Only Jesus is the head of His body, the ekklesia. 1 Cor. 11:3; Eph. 1:22; 5:23; Col. 1:18.

HYPOCRISY

Jesus hated the hypocrisy of the Pharisees. "All therefore whatsoever they bid you to observe, that observe and do; but do not do after their works, *for they say and do not.*" Matt. 23:3.

Hypocrisy is pretending something on the outside that does not exist on the inside. It is the pretense of virtues, principles, or beliefs that are not genuine. Jesus said the Pharisees were like whitewashed tombs which appear beautiful on the outside, but inside are full of dead men's bones and of all uncleanness. Matt. 23:27 NAS. He called them hypocrites. "Even so you also outwardly appear righteous unto men, but within you are full of hypocrisy and iniquity." Matt. 23:28. Again He accused them saying, "Woe unto you, scribes and Pharisees, *hypocrites!*" Matt. 23:14. What they said in keeping with the law of Moses was okay, but their failure to do what they expected others to do was not okay.

So it is in "THE Ministry" today. The pulpiteers may cry out for everyone else to be sexually pure, while pretending themselves to be pure when they are not. They may preach against smoking, drinking, cussin', and dancing, while pretending themselves to be holy when they are not. They may call for others to confess sins while they hide their own sins for fear of what others may think. They may condemn politicians for wrong doing while they continue to do what is most abominable to God—practicing their manipulations (witchcraft) upon "their" people.

The whole climate of *church* is clouded with hypocrisy. The *church* should be the one place we can go and feel safe enough to be ourselves, but it is not. We put on our masks and hide behind our Sunday morning smiles long enough to fulfill our obligations to God, feel good about doing it, and get to the cafeteria before the Methodists let out. Sunday morning *church* has little to do with how we live the rest of the week.

LEGALISM

Jesus hated the mean legalism of the Pharisees. *"They bind heavy burdens and grievous to be borne, and lay them on men's shoulders,* but they themselves will not move them with one of their fingers."* Matt. 23:4. Jesus hated their heavy-handedness over the people and how they imposed their laws upon everyone else.

Legalists in *churches* still bind people to *church* systems and orders, *church* buildings, *church* services and rituals, *church* giving, and *church* work—things that have nothing to do with Jesus or the Kingdom of God. People are made to feel guilty and unspiritual if they do not go to *church*.

Keeping the Sabbath was one such issue between Jesus and the Pharisees. Some legalists still make an issue of keeping the Sabbath day holy according to how they think it ought to be observed. They want to make Sunday (sometimes erroneously called "the Sabbath") the day of rest even though for them it is far from a day of rest—it is their high day of *church* works.

We do not keep the Sabbath by going to *church* on Sunday or by napping all day Sunday. We keep God's law by entering into Jesus through faith. Jesus is our Sabbath rest. Heb. 4. He is our righteousness. Jesus is not looking for a people who will keep the Sabbath day holy. He is looking for a people who will keep themselves holy (separated). Keeping the Sabbath day is not how we keep ourselves holy.

Holiness is the work of God's Holy Spirit in us, separating us from the love of the world. Holiness is a change of nature from within us as the result of God's work in us. It is not what we do outwardly, but who we are inwardly that matters to God. We are as phony as the Pharisees if we think our righteousness could ever depend upon what we do outwardly—the clothes we wear, the way we fix our hair, the food we eat or don't eat, the way we worship, or going to *church*. We live, move, and have our being in Jesus every moment of every day. (See the chapter on Legalism.)

RECOGNITION SEEKERS

Jesus hated the Pharisees' desire for recognition and how they pursued admiration for themselves. *"But all their works they do to be seen of men.* They make broad their phylacteries, and enlarge the borders of their garments."* Matt. 23:5. (Phylacteries were small leather boxes that the Pharisees strapped on their foreheads containing quotations from the first five books of the Bible).

The Nicolaitans in many *church* traditions today are enticed by their own lusts for self-importance to wear clerical collars, vestments, robes with academic stripes on their sleeves, and other such appointments to distinguish themselves from "the laity." A cardinal in the Roman Catholic *church* is addressed by saying, "His Eminence" or "Your Eminence." Such veneration of men smacks insult to God. Jesus called His disciples to Him and said to them as He would say today, "If any man desires to be first, the same shall be last of all, and servant of all." Mark 9:35.

PREEMINENCE

Jesus hated the self-inflated desire of the Pharisees to be above others. They *"love the uppermost rooms at feasts"* (the inner circle), *"and the chief seats in the synagogues"* (sitting on the platform). Matt. 23:6.

Preeminence is that air of self-importance within the present-day Nicolaitans that makes them want to be top dog in the system. They want to sit on the platform in bishop's chairs, making a difference between them and the people. Pastors give other pastors these places of prominence, because they love it for themselves.

It is that air of self-importance within them that causes them to gloat in their plans, programs, methods, organizations, building projects, heritage, traditions, statistics, and doctrines in order that they might be honored and recognized.

It is that air of self-importance within them to draw up organizational charts, pyramiding themselves at the top.

It is that air of self-importance within them that wants the bigger *church* and better salaries. They spare no politics to obtain them.

It is that air of self-importance within them that causes them to "sermonize" and wax eloquent from their pulpits in order to be highly esteemed of men.

It is that air of self-importance within them that wants to acquire knowledge, write books out of their own intellect, and achieve great things in order to be acclaimed of men. They hold their educated professionalism over the heads of the "laity," making themselves out to be one of the indisputable authorities in biblical and ecclesiastical matters. This is the tyranny of the clergy.

It is that air of self-importance within them that focuses upon the externals rather than upon the internals. They are preoccupied with building a kingdom for Self rather than building the Kingdom of God. They build *church* systems and *church* buildings rather than people. Worse yet, they confuse the one for the other.

It is that air of self-importance within them that compels them to pack their bags and run when the wolves of dissension nip at the heels of the flock. They are hirelings.

It is that air of self-importance within them that causes them to forget that they, too, are sheep under the staff of the Good Shepherd. Such pride and haughtiness makes them think more highly of themselves than they ought to think.

POSITION SEEKING

Jesus hated their desire for position. They love "greetings in the markets, *and to be called of men, Rabbi, Rabbi.*" Jesus continued to exhort them saying, "but do not be called Rabbi, for one is your Master, even Christ; and all you are brothers. And do not call man your father upon the earth, for one is your Father who is in heaven. Neither be called masters, for one is your Master, even Christ." Matt. 23:7-10.

The present-day Nicolaitan attitude is seen in that air of self-importance within them that wants to be called Pope, Your Eminence, Cardinal, Bishop, Father, Reverend, Reverend Mr., Pastor, and Minister with a capital M. The competition for recognition is so fierce today that many clergy persons want to be called "Doctor." Some of them have earned doctoral degrees and some have honorary degrees, but some have purchased phony degrees. They bestow titles upon each other within the system. They politic for places of authority and seek to be hired by the largest congregation within their reach.

Insecure people in ministry get their strokes from being in the ministry. There they gain power, position, recognition, security, financial income, and their sense of significance. Mature believers find that Jesus alone is their all in all.

No such "one-up, one-down" positioning exists in the Kingdom of God. Jesus made it clear that true leaders were servants. True leaders do not exalt themselves.

REBELLION AND STUBBORNNESS

Jesus hated the rebellion and stubbornness of the Pharisees. "But woe unto you, scribes and Pharisees, hypocrites, *for you shut up the kingdom of heaven against men, for you neither go in yourselves neither suffer them who are entering to go in.*" Matt. 23:13.

Many of the Pharisees had to have known from their thorough knowledge of the scriptures that Jesus was Messiah. Too many coincidences existed between Old Testament prophecies and the events of Jesus' life and death for those to be ignored. They knew! But did not want to believe. (See John 9:39-41.) They had compromised with the world system in order to gain power, position, riches, and dominance. While many Pharisees believed and turned to Jesus, most of them did not. Those who did not believe hardened their hearts against the truth. They refused to enter in and hindered others from entering in as well.

Many leaders in the *church* system today should know that "their" membership is held hostage by the rigidity of their belief systems and governmental systems, but they refuse to set them free. They teach and preach *church, church* works, and *church* membership as "the way." They need commitment from their membership in order to build a kingdom for themselves.

People are stuck in those places. Those who run the *churches* invite us to stay put in their place forever and shame us for going from place to place. Those who remain in these places are served up the same day-old, worm-infested manna. Spiritual growth is minimal, if at all. Any growth one might experience is most likely experienced outside of and in spite of that place.

Spiritual growth is, in reality, a spiritual journey. It is a journey that answers the call of Jesus, "Come, follow Me." "But Lord, let me first go bury my father." To which He still replies, "Let the dead bury the dead." Luke 9:59-60. If you find yourself in a dead place, get up and follow the Way, Jesus. Jesus is the Way, not a place. If we are to follow Jesus, we must not get stuck in a place. *Church* as we know it today is a roadblock to Jesus.

DEVOURING OTHERS

Jesus hated the way the Pharisees took advantage of widows. "Woe unto you, scribes and Pharisees, hypocrites! *for you devour widows' houses,* and for a pretense make long prayers; therefore, you shall receive the greater damnation." Matt. 23:14. Pharisees are takers, not givers, though they pretend to be giving something in return for offerings and donations.

This practice occurs everyday on so-called "Christian" television and radio. Great promises are made by televangelists to their fleeceable viewers who send them contributions. "Send me a donation of $50 and I will send you this anointing oil from Israel." The "Jesus" junk they offer is ridiculous. Bracelets, special study Bibles, books, healing cloths. Some will promise to pray for you or send you a book if you send them a donation. What if you do not? Are they still willing to pray for you and send the book? These gimmicks are used to increase their data and support base.

Kathleen was the widow of a benevolent man. After his death, she felt obligated to continue his level of generosity though she could not afford to do so. Knowing her vulnerability, the president of a seminary persuaded her to give an extraordinary contribution to his institution. It was a feather in his hat. She was a devout believer and assumed that her contribution was advancing the cause of Christ. Little did she know that this school was corrupting the faith of young men and women with their liberal, anti-Christ curriculum. He devoured her house.

Rather than devouring widow's houses, we should set our hearts upon devouring Jesus. Jesus said, "Except you eat the flesh of the Son of man, and drink His blood, you have no life in you...He who eats My flesh and drinks My blood dwells in Me, and I in him.." John 6:53,56. He alone has the words of eternal life. John 6:67-68.

PROSELYTIZING

Jesus hated how the Pharisees proselytized converts to Judaism. "Woe unto you, scribes and Pharisees, hypocrites! *for you compass sea and land to make one proselyte [convert to Judaism], and when he is made, you make him twofold more the child of hell than yourselves."* Matt. 23: 15.

A proselyte is a person who has been converted from their religion, faith, sect, or party to that of the one proselytizing them. The Pharisees were not doing others a favor by converting them to Judaism. Rather than bringing others to a faith in and relationship with Yahweh (God), they brought them to their religious observances of traditions, days, and rituals; thus implying, "This is the way, walk in it." In so doing, they put others under bondage to their law. Their motivation was to increase their own sphere of influence.

As with the Pharisees in Jesus' time, present-day Nicolaitans lead their converts to believe that salvation is assured by being associated with their form of religion. In so doing, they preach "another Jesus" and make their converts twice the children of hell as themselves.

Jesus came to set men free. Binding others to our religious practices is an offense to Him. We are to join people to Jesus in order to set them free. "If the Son therefore shall make you free, you shall be free indeed." John 8:36.

SELF-RIGHTEOUS

Jesus hated the snobbish self-righteousness of the Pharisees. "Woe to you scribes and Pharisees, hypocrites, *for you pay tithes of mint and anise and cummin, and have omitted the weightier matters of the law: judgment, mercy, and faith.* These you ought to have done and not left the other undone." Matt. 23:23. They kept the letter of the law: tithing "mint and anise and cummin," but knew nothing of the spirit of the law: "judgment, mercy, and faith." They thought by keeping the letter of the law, they would attain righteousness by the works of Self.

Self-righteousness is thinking that our righteousness has something to do with how well we perform. It suggests that we can appease God by being good or doing good works, by keeping the law, or such foolish things as fulfilling our Sunday morning obligation. The Pharisees kept the law in order to be saved by the law. Paul expressly stated that "the letter kills, but the Spirit gives life." 2 Cor. 3:6. They knew the law, but did not know the Spirit of the law.

Self-righteous persons can be legalistic, prideful, arrogant, haughty, religious, pious, hateful, restrictive, judgmental, critical, rude, preachy, mean, dangerous, and lacking in mercy, compassion, kindness, and generosity. By contrast, the fruit of the Spirit is love, joy, peace, long-suffering, gentleness, goodness, faith, meekness, and self-control. Gal. 5:22-23.

Our righteousness is not God's righteousness. "Ours." "His." See the difference?! His righteousness can be ours only through faith in Christ, but our attempts at righteousness can never be His. Jesus is the righteousness of God. He alone fulfilled all the law and the prophets. Matt. 5:17. Philippians 3:9 reminds us that we are to be found in Christ, not having our own righteousness, which is of the law, but that which is through faith in Christ.

We are the righteousness of God in Christ. 2 Cor. 5:21. It does not say we "will be," "we should be," or "we almost are," it says "we are." It has to do with *being* and not with *doing*. We *are* because Jesus made us to be who we are in Him through His own finished work on the cross. There is nothing in fallen, sinful man that has the potential to save himself or to be good enough for God to put his saving stamp of approval upon him.

MURDER

Jesus hated the murderous hearts of the Pharisees. "Woe to you scribes and Pharisees, hypocrites, because you build the tombs of the prophets, and garnish the sepulchers of the righteous and say, 'If we had been in the days of our fathers, we would not have been partakers with them in the blood of the prophets.' Wherefore you are witnesses unto yourselves, *that you are the children of them who killed the prophets.*" Matt. 23:29-31. Moreover, Jesus predicted that they would kill and crucify some of the prophets, wise men, and scribes that He would be sending. "And some of them you shall scourge in your synagogues, and persecute them from city to city; that upon you may come all the righteous blood shed upon earth." Matt. 23:34-35.

Jesus said to the unbelieving Jews in John 8:44, "You are of your father the devil, and the lusts [desires] of your father you will do. He was a murderer from the beginning, and abode not in the truth, because there is no truth in him." If Jesus said that the devil was a murderer and that the unbelieving Jews were his sons, the implication was that they, too, were murderers. Jesus had previously established that they sought to kill Him. John 8:31.

If they could, the unrepentant Pharisees in the *church* system today would kill those who threaten to dethrone them from their little empires. They are the tares that have grown up among the wheat. In Matthew 13:24-30, Jesus said it would be that way.

Nicolaitans today spiritually slaughter the sheep of God when they use them for their personal and sordid gain.

I went to a seminary as a young man in the ministry. I was taught that the miracles were not real and that much of what was told in the Old Testament were myths. I was taught religion, but religion had no life. I was young, impressionable, and ungrounded in the word and Spirit. Rather than being built up in faith, I became spiritually bankrupt. Eventually, I became a professed atheist until my radical conversion years later.

We are instructed in the scriptures to turn away from those who have the form of godliness, but deny its power. 2 Tim. 3:5.

These present-day Nicolaitans, who bear the marks of the Pharisees, are the doorkeepers in spiritual Babylon. Babylon is the Great Mother of Harlots. Rev. 17:5. Her other name is Jezebel. She is the puppeteer behind the stage that pulls the strings of the Nicolaitans in the *churches* today.

Chapter 11

Jezebel

*J*esus said to the believers at Thyatira, "I have a few things against you." That should get one's attention. Why did He say that? "Because you have suffered [allowed] that woman Jezebel, who calls herself a prophetess, to teach and seduce my servants to commit fornication, and to eat things sacrificed to idols." Rev. 2:20. Who was "that woman Jezebel" and what did she do that Jesus would have had such contempt toward her?

A SPIRITUAL CONDITION

Jezebel in Thyatira may have been a real person among the called-out-ones there and may have actually been engaging in sexual immorality. She may have been actually drawing others into her ways. Such is not out of the question since adultery goes on in the *churches* today. It always has. Even so, something far more engaging, far more spiritually significant, for which the Lord showed contempt, was going on there.

The "Jezebel spirit" in Thyatira represented a spiritual condition in the hearts of some of the called-out-ones there. Ahab's Jezebel in the Old Testament defines what this Jezebel spirit is by her life and reputation. She was controlling and manipulative and practiced witchcraft and harlotry.

Spiritual harlotry is seeking anything for Self. It is the flesh hungering to enhance itself. We all have harlot hearts and are easily deceived. When this idolatrous harlotry is brought into our assembly life as the body of Christ, we have the Jezebel spirit in operation. Our idolatry and spiritual harlotry may not be so blatant as hers, but is just as much a hindrance to having an intimate relationship with our Lord.

This Jezebel in Thyatira and this "MYSTERY, BABYLON THE GREAT, THE MOTHER OF HARLOTS AND ABOMINATIONS OF THE EARTH" (Rev. 17:1-6) represent the same spiritual condition—idolatry and spiritual harlotry (fornication). Jezebel in Thyatira taught and seduced the Lord's servants to commit fornication, and to eat things sacrificed to idols. This harlot of Revelation 17 is pictured as the great whore that sat "upon many waters with whom the kings of the earth have committed fornication, and the inhabitants of the earth have been made drunk with the wine of her fornication." She was "drunk with the blood of the saints, and with the blood of the martyrs of Jesus."

THE JEZEBEL SPIRIT DEFINED

The Jezebel-harlot spirit is seeking anything for Self. It is the idolatry of Self—self-love. Philippians 2:21 reads, "For all seek their own, not the things which are Jesus Christ's." Whoever seeks his own is into self-love. self-love is idolatry, and all idolatry is spiritual harlotry. Our sin nature is prone to self-love and his condition is made worse by the enticement of demonic spirits.

The harlot spirit is present anytime we try to build something in the flesh for Self. In contrast, the Holy Spirit is present when we set our hearts to build only for Him and by Him. We deceive ourselves when we think that our great *church* building programs are for Him. They are not. They are for Self. Many well-meaning, but ill-informed Christians try to exploit the Holy Spirit to advance themselves. Many fake the presence of the Holy Spirit to make their *church* or their services look good. This is wrong. We have not been given the Holy Spirit to make the harlot look good.

The Jezebel spirit is further defined by her deeds.

SHE LEADS GOD'S SERVANTS ASTRAY

The Jezebel spirit leads astray God's bond-servants, those who willingly commit to serving Christ.

The Jezebel of Thyatira led people astray through her doctrine—the things she taught. The Lord said, "But to you I say, and to the rest in Thyatira, as many as *have not this doctrine [teaching]...*" Rev. 2:24. She was violating their minds and spirituality with false teachings; namely, those teachings that would exalt Self, especially herself that she might have the rule over them. In this, she was causing them to eat things sacrificed to idols. The idols in this case was Self. All idolatry stems from the love of Self.

Through her doctrines she did the same thing Balaam was found guilty of doing. The use of this expression "eating things sacrificed to idols" links her to Balaam. Knowing who Balaam was and what he did explained who the Nicolaitans were and now explains who "that woman Jezebel" was. They all sought something for Self in order to gain dominance over the people.

Eating things sacrificed to idols is what we do when we allow the old, arrogant, self-centered, self-promoting man of flesh and sin to rule rather than allowing the Holy Spirit to rule. It is the lordship of the harlot instead of the lordship of Jesus Christ.

Some at Thyatira were beguiled by the self-seeking, self-promoting "doctrine" advanced by "that woman Jezebel." These doctrines later influenced the rise of the clergy system. It was a system of men's self-seeking traditions based on power, position, pomp, preeminence, riches, and domination.

Those in the *churches* today who violate God's sheep in order to increase themselves in power, position, and domination are, likewise, causing the sheep to eat things sacrificed to idols—the idols of self-glorification.

SHE INCITES BAAL WORSHIP

It is not coincidental that the woman in Revelation chapter 2 is named Jezebel, or that the woman in Revelation chapter 17 is called MOTHER OF HARLOTS. There could be no more perfect picture of all that is an abomination to God than the Jezebel of 1 Kings 16 who married Ahab, king of Israel. As we investigate her life and practices, we shall surely be convinced that she serves as a symbolic type of the harlot spirit in the *church* system that was to come.

Jezebel was a Phoenician princess, the daughter of Ethbaal, King of Tyre, of the Sidonians. Ahab, King of Israel, married her. The scriptures reads, "And it came to pass, as if it had been a light thing for him to walk in the sins of Jeroboam the son of Nebat, that he [Ahab] took to wife Jezebel...and went and served Baal, and worshipped him." 1 Kings 16:31. In this, Ahab "did more to provoke the LORD God of Israel to anger than all the kings of Israel that were before him." 1 Kings 16:33. She led Ahab to worship Baal.

Baal means "possessor" and was the god of the increase of flocks, crops, and families. It might be defined in present-day terms as "greed." Baal worship is self-worship and characterized by the love of the world: the lust for power, position, riches, and domination much like what we see throughout the history of the *church* and its system of clergy.

If the Jezebel spirit can succeed in getting God's bond-servants to worship other gods, to get their eyes off of Jesus and onto themselves, she will have caused them to commit spiritual fornication and to eat things sacrificed to idols. She will have caused them to commit sins that are an abomination to God.

When we lift up this Thing we call *church* and join people to *it*, we turn their hearts away from the one who should be their first and only love, Jesus Christ.

SHE CONSULTS THE PROPHETS OF BAAL

The Jezebel spirit consults the prophets of Baal. The prophets of Baal say things that appeal to and entice the desires of the flesh.

Ahab's Jezebel had her own prophets of Baal. She allowed the prophets of Baal to eat at her table. 1 Kings 18:19. They tickled her ears by telling her what she wanted to hear. She wanted to hear whatever she thought might bring an increase of power, control, and grandeur to herself.

Such was the case with Ahab when he joined Jehoshaphat in war against the king of Syria over Ramoth in Gilead. Jehoshaphat pleaded with Ahab to inquire of the Lord before they went to battle. Ahab gathered about four hundred of the prophets of Baal, and they told him to proceed, assuring him that the Lord would deliver him. It was already in his heart to do this thing, so they told him what he wanted to hear. Jehoshaphat asked, "Is there not a prophet of the Lord that we might inquire of him?" No doubt Ahab bristled at this suggestion. Ahab knew the prophet Micaiah but told Jehoshaphat, "I hate him; for he does not prophesy good concerning me, but evil." Nevertheless, Micaiah was consulted and told Ahab the same thing his lying prophets had told him, "Go, and prosper: for the LORD shall deliver it into the hand of the king." Ahab knew he was not speaking the word of the Lord and commanded him to speak the truth. So he did. "I saw all Israel scattered upon the hills, as sheep that have not a shepherd." 2 Chronicles 18:22 adds, "and the LORD has declared disaster against you." Fascinating! Ahab knew Micaiah was not speaking truth, he knew it was not God's will to go to battle, but he did it anyway, bringing about his own destruction. 1 Kings 22.

The "Ahabs" in the *churches* today surround themselves with "yes" men. They will continue to bow down to their own Baals and consult with their own prophets of Baal as long as they are addicted to bigger, better, and more. Bigger, better, and more of anything. Bigger, better, and more of everything. Bigger *church* buildings. Better salaries. More members. Greater offerings. Increased honor, recognition, and reputation. Even when they know this is leading to their destruction, their insatiable appetite for increase drives them on. They do it anyway.

SHE KILLS THE PROPHETS OF GOD

The Jezebel spirit kills the prophets of God.

Ahab's Jezebel is noted for having killed the prophets of the Lord. 1 Kings 18:4,13. The Lord avenged the blood of His servants the prophets and the blood of all the servants of the Lord at the hand of

Jezebel (2 Kings 9:7) by anointing Jehu, one of Ahab's captains, to be the King of Israel and instructing him to kill the house of Ahab.

Ahab's Jezebel and THE MOTHER OF HARLOTS shared this reputation: they killed the prophets of God. Revelation 17:6 describes the woman as being "drunken with the blood of the saints, and with the blood of the martyrs of Jesus." Revelation 18:24 reads that "in her was found the blood of prophets, and of saints and of all that were slain upon the earth."

Her powers go beyond that of a conniving woman. She was a partner with the powers of darkness—one to shun, one from whom to run. Elijah had sense enough to know this. He had won a mighty victory for the Lord on Mount Carmel. Fire came down from heaven at his petition and consumed the altars of Jezebel's prophets. Then Elijah slew all 450 of her prophets with the sword at the Brook Kishon. 1 Kings 18:20-40. Such bravery! Such confidence in God! Then, when "that woman Jezebel" threatened to do to him what he had done to her prophets, he ran for his life and wisely so. He recognized the depth of evil in her. He fled a day's journey into the wilderness, sat down under a juniper tree, and pleaded with the Lord to take his life. 1 Kings 19:1-4.

This spirit in Jezebel was already scheming in Israel during the time of the Judges when Samson foolishly gave himself to Delilah, a woman in the Valley of Sorek. She enticed him to give away the secret of his strength, which cost him his strength, his freedom, his eyesight, and eventually his life. Judg. 16:4-22.

John the Baptist, the prophet, fell victim to this heinous spirit. Matt. 14:1-12. John had condemned Herod for taking his brother's wife, Herodias. Herod wanted to put John to death, but feared the multitude who considered John to be a prophet. On the occasion of Herod's birthday, the daughter of Herodias danced before his illustrious birthday crowd. Her performance was so pleasing that Herod foolishly offered her anything she wished up to half of his kingdom. Her mother wasted no time prompting her to ask for the head of John. The Bible says that Herod was sorry but had boasted his pledge in the hearing of all present and could not squirm his way out of it. John's head fell, and the Jezebel spirit had claimed the life of another prophet of God.

If Jezebel cannot kill the prophet of God outright, she will try to seduce him into some immoral, illegal, or unscrupulous act in order to derail him. The story of Joseph and Potiphar's wife is the classic, scriptural example of this. Though he had been bought as a slave, Joseph found favor with Potiphar, and God blessed Potiphar because of Joseph's presence in his house. Potiphar entrusted the management of his household and wealth to Joseph. Potipher's wife was a different matter. She had sexual designs on Joseph and tried to entice him into her bedroom. Joseph, being a man of integrity, refused her enticements. She snared him anyway. She grabbed his garment from him as he fled from her, took the garment to Potiphar, and falsely accused him of trying to have sex with her. Though Potiphar imprisoned him, the Jezebel spirit ultimately failed, for God used Joseph's imprisonment to lead him to his destiny—the seat of high honor and trust in Pharaoh's house. Gen. 39:7-20.

Proverbs 5:1-8 is a warning to the natural man that applies to the spiritual man as well. "My son, attend unto my wisdom, and bow your ear to my understanding: That you may regard discretion, and that your lips may keep knowledge. For the lips of a strange woman drop as an honeycomb, and her mouth is smoother than oil: but her end is bitter as wormwood, sharp as a two-edged sword. Her feet go down to death; her steps take hold on hell. Lest you should ponder the path of life, her ways are moveable, that you cannot know them. Hear me now therefore, O you children, and depart not from the words of my mouth. Remove your way far from her, and come not near the door of her house."

The Jezebel spirit in the *churches* today is no less a threat to the servants of God. Many true and godly servants of Christ have been spiritually and emotionally damaged and disfellowshipped from the *churches* because they sought to follow the leading of the Holy Spirit against the interest of their rigid denominational traditions. Additionally, as Bob Hughey points out, "The harlot steals affection, time, energy, financial resources, and seed away from the bride. Jesus will never give His seed to the harlot." Just as the physical seed of humans is the sperm; so is the spiritual seed the word of God. His word is for His bride. We are to receive with meekness the implanted word, which is able to save our souls. James 1:21b.

SHE DESTROYS THE ROYAL OFFSPRING OF DAVID

This Jezebel spirit is murderous and would try to alter world history. She stops at nothing to destroy God's inheritance, attempting to kill even the royal offspring from King David to King Jesus.

Jezebel and Ahab had a daughter named Athaliah who married Jehoram, king of Judah. After he died, Athaliah's son, Ahaziah, became king in Judah but was killed by Jehu. When Athaliah saw that her son was dead, she arose, began to kill all the royal offspring from the house of Judah, seized the throne for herself, and reigned for six years. She inherited her mother's demon.

Athaliah succeeded in killing all the royal offspring except for Joash. Jehoshabeath, the daughter of king Ahaziah, hid Joash from the other sons who were being killed. Joash was later crowned king of Judah by the congregation of Levites and chief fathers of Israel under the leadership of Jehoiada, a priest.

When Athaliah heard the commotion surrounding the crowning ceremony of Joash, she tore her clothes and shouted, "Treason! Treason!" Johoiada ordered that she be taken outside the Temple and put to death. 2 Kings 8:25-11:20 or 2 Chron. 22-23.

We realize the magnitude of this historical event when we remember that Jesus, the Messiah, was to be a descendent of David. 1 Chron. 17:11-12. Had Joash himself been murdered with the rest of the royal offspring from David, this would have interrupted that divine lineage.

As we come to the end of the age we find Satan, the real influence that empowers the Jezebel spirit, once again attempting to destroy the royal offspring of David. All who are the called, chosen, and faithful (Rev. 17:14) are the malechild of Revelation 12:1-5 who is to rule the nations with a rod of iron, whom the dragon attempts to devour. This malechild is a corporate son, bearing the image of the Son, whom the Holy Spirit will manifest in these last days.

The Jezebel spirit attempts to destroy the spirit of Sonship when it is preached, perverts the revelation when it comes forth, and holds many people hostage to the religious systems of men.

SHE SITS AS QUEEN

The Jezebel spirit seeks to position herself as queen.

Ahab's Jezebel ruled surreptitiously. She was the power behind the throne. The Jezebel spirit historically has been acting in stealth, but the Holy Spirit reveals that she will actually position herself openly upon the throne just as did Athaliah. "How much she has glorified herself...for she says in her heart, 'I sit as a queen...'" Rev. 18:7. It is already coming to pass not only in the *church* but in all areas of life; she will sit as queen before the end of the age.

The Jezebel spirit despises the authority of the man. She is driven to usurp the headship of her husband—taking over what God has given him to do. She answers for him, makes decisions for him, and manipulates him to get her way. She uses sex, crying, sulking, conniving, self-pity, and threats to achieve what she wants. This is vividly illustrated in the next chapter on Naboth.

The Jezebel spirit wants more than anything to rule in the *churches* and to rule over God's elect. She targets the leadership when she can. The elders of a small city fellowship would meet, pray, and agree together on the direction they believed the Lord was leading. The next time they met, elder John often had reversed his position. Why? He went home, talked it over with his wife, and if it did not comply with her agenda, she persuaded him to change his mind. She ruled him; thereby, she controlled most of what happened in this fellowship through him. He was an Ahab and she was a Jezebel.

Jezebel is driven by ambition and is characterized by the headship of the woman. The Holy Spirit established God's order for headship through Paul. He wrote, "But I would have you know, that the head of every man is Christ; and the head of the woman is the man; and the head of Christ is God." 1 Cor. 11:2.

This principle of headship is not a question of citizenship or greatness. It certainly does not call for abusive behavior on the part of the husband nor blind obedience on the part of the wife. It is a matter of jurisdiction. It is a responsibility each man has before his Head, Christ, to properly love and cover his wife. Coach Bill McCartney spoke profoundly on the NBC Today Show, November 19, 1997, saying, "Every man's calling is to bring his wife to splendor." A godly man will be a true shepherd over his household. He will lead, feed, heal, and tend to them.

Women who usurp their coverings of headship open themselves up to deceiving spirits. 1 Cor. 11:10. Women who become the "power behind the throne" or in any sense begin to exercise authority over their husbands open themselves up to a Jezebel spirit. 1 Cor. 2:12-14. The headship of women is out of order and dangerous. It will lead God's bond-servants astray.

Babylonian-based *churches* are powered by the secret influences of Jezebel spirits, and the Ahabs are pawns in their hands. These spirits will be available and functioning when this harlot *church* system is in place. This idolatrous system of self-worship attracts demons like flies to a picnic.

SHE IS CAST DOWN IN A DAY

THE MOTHER OF HARLOTS is in contrast to the bride in Revelation 19:7-9. This counterfeit is the mother of the abominations of the earth. She is an abomination to the Lord and will be cast down in a day. Her glory already pales with the rising glory of God's true and holy bride.

A striking similarity exists between Ahab's Jezebel and THE MOTHER OF HARLOTS in how they are terminated.

2 Kings 9:30-33 narrates how Ahab's Jezebel died. Jehu had been anointed to replace Jehoram as the king of Israel and was

given the charge to slay the whole house of Ahab, including Jezebel. When Jehu came to Jezreel, he found Jezebel looking through a window. Upon his command, some eunuchs threw her down and some of her blood was sprinkled on the wall and on the horses. Jehu trod her under foot. They later went out to bury her, but the dogs had eaten all of her except her skull, feet, and the palms of her hands just as Elisha had prophesied. 1 Kings 21:23.

Revelation 18:2 records, "Fallen, fallen is Babylon the great!" Verse 8 reads: "For this reason in one day her plagues will come…" Verse 10: "Woe, woe, the great city, Babylon, the strong city! For in one hour your judgment has come." Verse 17: "…for in one hour such great wealth has been laid waste!" Verse 21: "and a strong angel took up a stone like a great millstone and threw it into the sea, saying, 'Thus will Babylon, the great city, be thrown down with violence, and will not be found any longer.'"

The second angel said in Revelation 14:8, "Babylon is fallen, is fallen, that great city, because she made all nations drink of the wine of the wrath of her fornication."

Then one of the seven angels in Revelation 17:1-2 said, "Come here, I will show you the judgment of the great whore who sits upon many waters: with whom the kings of the earth have committed fornication, and the inhabitants of the earth have been made drunk with the wine of her fornication."

Finally, in Revelation 19:1-2, John "heard a great voice of much people in heaven, saying, 'Alleluia; Salvation, and glory, and honor, and power, unto the Lord our God: For true and righteous are His judgments: for He has judged the great whore, which corrupted the earth with her fornication…'"

This idolatrous system of men's traditions, bundled in this Thing we call *church* and typified by the Jezebel spirit is destined to be destroyed. Revelation 2:21-24 tells the rest of the story. "And I gave her [Jezebel] space to repent of her fornication; and she repented not. Behold, I will cast her into a bed, and them that commit adultery with her into great tribulation, except they repent of their deeds. And I will kill her children with death; and all the *assemblies* of *called-out-ones* shall know that I am He who searches the minds and hearts: and I will give unto every one of you according to your works. But unto you I say, and unto the rest in Thyatira, as many as have not this doctrine, and which have not known the depths of Satan, as they speak; I will put upon you none other burden."

The rule of the carnal mind in the *church* is the Babylonian captivity of the *church*. The Nicolaitans are the doorkeepers and Jezebel rules behind the scenes. She is a black widow spider who weaves her web of seduction and deceit to trap whom she can.

And so it happened to Naboth. He, too, was caught in her snare.

*I*t was a choice day for Naboth as he strolled through his vineyard tasting his dew-covered grapes in the still of the morning. "A good crop this year," he thought to himself, smiling and nodding his head in agreement. 1 Kings 21 (with a little of my own imagination).

The eastern sun blinded Naboth's view of Ahab, the king of Israel, who was nervously approaching him. Ahab was out early that morning. He had something on his mind. His palace was next door to Naboth's vineyard.

"Oh!" Naboth was startled by Ahab. "I didn't hear you coming."

Ahab wasted no time in making his offer to Naboth. "Give me your vineyard so I can have a vegetable garden next to the palace here. I will give you a better vineyard somewhere else, or if you prefer, I will give you its worth in money."

Naboth took a step back. He could not believe what was being asked of him. He didn't need time to think about it. It blurted right out of his mouth. "The LORD forbid me that I should give the inheritance of my fathers to you." 1 Kings 21:3.

Ahab's countenance fell. His heart was set on getting this piece of property from Naboth. Heart sickened, he went into his house, laid down on his bed, turned his face away, and had a pity-party.

Jezebel found Ahab sulking and asked, "Why are you so down that you can't even eat?"

"Naboth won't give me his vineyard," he whined.

She rose to the occasion and said what any good Jezebel would say in a situation like this. "Are you not the authority over Israel? Get up! Eat! Be merry! I'll take care of this. I will give you Naboth's vineyard."

Ahab did what any good Ahab would do. He did what she told him to do and never questioned how she planned on getting Naboth's vineyard. A friend of mine saw it this way: "He did not wish to know for fear that he might find her plans disagreeable. These Ahabs are not stupid. They often live vicariously through their Jezebels."

She wasted no time. Her disregard for Naboth was obvious. This was her opportunity to gain more power and authority for herself. She achieved her goal by ruling covertly through her husband. She was the voice behind him.

She whisked past the servants outside of Ahab's bedroom, tossed her shawl over her shoulder, marched toward the royal office, pulled out a piece of parchment, and began to write letters to the elders and nobles who lived in the city. She forged Ahab's name on them, poured wax beside his name, and carefully sealed the letters with his signet ring.

"Proclaim a fast," she wrote, "and set Naboth on high among the people: and set two worthless men before him to bear witness against him, saying, 'You blasphemed God and the king.' Then carry him out, and stone him, that he may die."

I wonder! Did the men of the city, those elders and nobles, know that Jezebel was the author of this murderous scheme? Did they pretend not to know? Did they not know the good reputation of Naboth and that this was a fabrication against him? Regardless—being the *yes* men that they were—they did what the royal palace asked them to do. They held their kangaroo court, sentenced a good man on the word of two scoundrels, and stoned him to death.

Word quickly returned to Jezebel that Naboth was dead. She ran into Ahab's chambers, yanked the covers from off his head, and shouted, "Get up! Take possession of Naboth's vineyard. He is no longer alive, but is dead."

Still, no questions asked. The evil deed was done. Ahab and Jezebel had what they wanted. Or so they thought.

THE SYMBOLS

This story reads like a parable and has striking similarities to the circumstances surrounding the death of Jesus. It continues to speak to the present condition in the *church*. Reading about Naboth as a parable further exposes the nature, deeds, teachings, and work of the Nicolaitans and the Jezebel spirit. Ahab particularly further defines the Nicolaitan spirit.

Nearly every person, place, and part in this story has symbolic meaning. Naboth's name means "sprout." As such, he is a type of Jesus, the root of Jesse. He lived in Jezreel which means "God sows." Jezreel is a type of the Kingdom of God wherein God sows the good seed of the word to bring forth His vineyard. Naboth's vineyard represents the general assembly of called-out-ones, which is the body of Christ—all those who are born from above by the eternal seed in Christ. Jesus is the true vine, the Father is the vinedresser, and we are the branches. We abide in Him and He abides in us. John 15:1-8. We are the fruit of that vine as well.

We must know that the enemy of our faith seeks to steal, kill, and destroy (John 10:10)—doing whatever it takes to claim God's vineyard for himself.

THE INHERITANCE

Naboth was horrified at Ahab's insult. His vineyard was more than a piece of real estate. It was the inheritance of his fathers. "The LORD forbid me that I should give the inheritance of my fathers to you," he told Ahab.

Listen for the double meaning here: "the inheritance *of* my fathers." What was taken from Naboth was taken from his forefathers as well. If the inheritance I leave for my children is stolen from them, it is stolen from me because it was *my* inheritance for them. It becomes a personal thing.

We as God's vineyard are His inheritance. Paul prayed for the Ephesians—a prayer to which we can all lay claim—"that the God of our Lord Jesus Christ, the Father of glory, may give to you the spirit of wisdom and revelation in the knowledge of Him: that the eyes of your understanding may be enlightened; that you may know what is the hope of His calling, and what are the riches of the glory of *His inheritance* in the saints." Eph. 1:18.

Likewise, we have our inheritance in Him. Ephesians 1:11 says that we have obtained an inheritance through Christ. Colossians 1:12 adds that we are partakers of the inheritance of the saints in light. Hebrews 9:15 assures us that we have the promise of the eternal inheritance. 1 Peter 1:3-4 declares that we have been born again from the dead to a lively hope by the resurrection of Jesus Christ that leaves us an incorruptible and undefiled inheritance that will not fade away. It is reserved in heaven. Our redemption in Christ Jesus is a wonderful inheritance for us. It is what God wants for us. Likewise, our redemption is an inheritance for God. It is what God wants for Himself. It, too, is a very personal thing with Him.

Israel of old was given an inheritance of land. They were to take it for themselves and for God. Spiritually speaking, we also have been given a land to possess for ourselves and for God. Our land is our souls; that is, our minds, wills, and emotions. We have a spiritual inheritance of righteousness, peace, and joy in the Holy Ghost; of redemption, sanctification, and glorification; of becoming the sons of God through obedience. For we are the heirs of God and joint-heirs with Christ. Rom. 8:17. We get what God wants for us, and

God gets what He must have from us. We mutually benefit.

It is little wonder, then, that Satan would pull the strings on his Ahab marionettes to rob us and God of our inheritance. Satan, like Ahab, wants God's vineyard for himself. His primary mission in our lives is to destroy those of us who are heirs and joint-heirs with Christ. False shepherds sneak into the fold as wolves in sheep's clothing to claim God's inheritance for themselves. Pastors refer to congregations as *their* people. We identify a body of believers as "Brother Bobby's" *church*. We cannot possess what God owns. We belong to one another in the kingdom of God, but we are never to own one another. We are His sheep and the sheep of His pasture.

Ahab wanted the vineyard for a vegetable garden and not for the grapes and wine it could produce. He wanted to change its character. The Ahabs of today change the character of God's holy vineyard. They clone others to look like themselves to satisfy their own agendas rather than permitting the Holy Spirit to conform others into the image of Jesus. Satan gains control of God's vineyard through the self-aggrandizing personalities of the heavy-handed Ahabs that rule the *churches*.

THE PROPOSITION

Ahab promised Naboth that he would replace his vineyard with a better one or give him the price in money for it. In a similar way, Satan tried to buy off Jesus when he came to Him in the wilderness, showed him all the kingdoms of the world, and told him that He could have all of them and their glory if He would only bow down and worship him.

Jesus answered the Devil, "Get behind me Satan: for it is written, 'You shall worship the Lord your God, and Him only shall you serve.'" Luke 4:5-8. Naboth answered Ahab by saying, "The LORD forbid me that I should give you the inheritance of my fathers." Had Jesus yielded to the temptation to sell out to Satan, there would have been no "inheritance in the saints." Eph. 1:18.

Ahab is a type of the clergy within the harlot *church* system— those who seek something for Self. Ahab-type ministries today must have a following in order to advance themselves in power, position, riches, and dominance. David Fitzpatrick maintains that the purpose of leadership is "to help train and equip people to work out the call of God that is on their lives...but today's church seems to flow too often in one direction—toward the center, continually gathering everyone's talents and gifts and using them to accomplish the goals of a few." He emphasizes: "I do not believe the life of the people should be consumed in helping a leader accomplish his goals in life." In bold simplicity he asserts, "We must release people, not possess them."[21]

THE PLOT

Jezebel's name means "unhusbanded." This means that she was an uncovered woman. A woman can be unmarried, yet covered; and she can be married, yet uncovered. The difference has to do with her having a submissive heart. Jezebel not only failed to submit to the headship of her husband, but usurped the headship of her husband. She ruled the roost. As such, she is a type of the harlot *church* system in which people are the heads and not Christ. Their *head*quarters are in cities rather than in the Kingdom of God. Through these systems the Jezebel spirit plots and schemes to accomplish its personal ambitions and agendas.

This happened to Jesus. Matthew 26:3-4 reads, "Then the chief priests and the elders of the people were gathered together in the court of the high priest, named Caiaphas; and they plotted together to seize Jesus by stealth, and kill him." We can well imagine that Jezebel spirit hovering over the Ahabs/Nicolaitans in Jesus' time, goading them to crucify the Son of the living God. Certainly, it was present.

As in the case of Naboth, there were two worthless men present to testify against Jesus. Matthew 26:59-61 documents it: "Now the chief priests and the whole Council kept trying to obtain false testimony against Jesus, in order that they might put Him to death; and they did not find any, even though many false witnesses came forward. But later on two came forward and said, 'This man stated, I am able to destroy the temple of God and to rebuild it in three days.'"

After they brought Jesus before Pilate, they began to accuse Him of misleading the nation and forbidding to pay taxes to Caesar and of saying that He was the Christ, a King. Luke 23:2. He was Christ and King, but their intent in saying so was evil. And, as in the case of Naboth, they even accused Him of blasphemy. Matt. 26:65.

The Pharisees, Sadducees, rulers, and elders of Judaism at the time of Christ had this political Ahab/Nicolaitan spirit in them. Remember that Nicolaitan means "conqueror of the people." John 11:47-48 bears witness to this. "Therefore the chief priests and the Pharisees convened a council, and were saying, 'What are we doing? For this man is performing many signs. If we let Him go on like

---

[21]David Fitzpatrick, *Issues of the Heart: Let My People Go* (Thompson Station, TN: Innercourt, 1992), 73-74.

this, all men will believe in Him, and the Romans will come and take away both our place and our nation.'"

THE EXECUTION

The plot against Naboth was executed as Jezebel scripted. The elders and nobles had surely known Naboth all their lives and had known that the accusations were false. Nevertheless, because of the intimidating influence of the Ahab and Jezebel spirits, they killed him anyway. They took Naboth outside of the city and stoned him to death.

In this same way, the religious leaders, with political endorsements, caused Jesus to be taken outside of the city walls of Jerusalem to a hill called Golgotha (meaning "place of a skull") and ordered that He be nailed onto a Roman cross. Mark 15:22.

The Ahabs and Nicolaitans in the *church* today still intimidate believers with fear; for example, they may tell them they will be out of God's will if they leave their *church*.

Hebrews 13:13 charges us saying, "Hence, let us go out to Him outside the camp, bearing His reproach." Going outside of the camp for us today is like coming out of the harlot *church* system. You cannot live a laid-down, Spirit-led life in *it*. You will either be controlled by those who rule *it* or by the Holy Spirit. *Church* membership is voluntary. If you have voluntarily placed yourself under false leadership such as we have in the harlot *church* system, you are under false headship. If, on the other hand, you permit yourself to be led by the Holy Spirit and that runs contrary to the agenda of the leadership in your *church*, you will most likely cause trouble. If those who rule *it* cannot control you, they will put you out, find ways to silence you, or at best, ignore you.

THE POSSESSION

After Naboth had been stoned, Jezebel aroused Ahab and told him to take possession of Naboth's vineyard. Possessiveness and ownership are main traits of the Nicolaitan and Jezebel spirits.

The takeover of Naboth's vineyard became Ahab and Jezebel's downfall, for God delivered His judgment against them. Likewise, the death of Jesus by the "Ahabs" of His day was their defeat. Jesus made it clear to the disciples that no man could take His life. He had the power to lay it down and to take it up again. John 10:18. Jesus laid down His life for His sheep. John 10:15.

The ancient story of Naboth, Ahab, and Jezebel had been given as a preview performance on the stage of history. Only the names of the characters were changed. 1 Kings 21:15-16 could just as well have read, "And it came about when the Jezebel spirit heard that Jesus and all of the apostles were dead, that it said to the Ahabs/Nicolaitans (clergymen), 'Arise, go down to the called-out-ones, to take possession of them.'" This is exactly what happened, and they have ruled the *churches* from the second century A.D. until now.

Balaam's strategy remains the same to this day: "If we cannot curse them, we will seduce them into the harlotry of Self." Whatever it takes, the Ahabs and Nicolaitans must possess "their own."

THE ELIJAH SPIRIT

This morning was different than the one when Naboth tasted the freshly ripened grapes from his vineyard. This morning Ahab had risen early to survey the plowed-up fields of Naboth's vineyard while Naboth's death still haunted every furrow of ground. Ahab could not care less. He had what he wanted, so he thought.

In stomped Elijah with the fire of God's anointing in his eyes. He wasted no time nor did he exchange pleasantries. "Have you killed and taken possession? This is what God says to you, 'In the place where dogs licked the blood of Naboth shall dogs lick your blood.'" 1 Kings 21:19.

Stumbling over his own ineptness, Ahab asked Elijah, "Did you find me, O enemy of mine?" The Ahabs will always view the true prophets of God as their enemies, for the true prophets do not say what the Ahabs want to hear.

"I found you," Elijah answered, "because you have sold yourself to work evil in the sight of the LORD." God declared through Elijah, moreover, that He would bring evil upon Ahab, cut off his posterity, and make his house like Jeroboam and Baasha for the way he had provoked the Lord to anger and made Israel to sin. And so it happened just as Elijah prophesied.

The Elijah spirit is being released today in part to speak judgment against the Ahabs and Jezebels who teach and seduce God's servants to commit fornication and to eat things sacrificed to idols. Rev. 2:20. How we give our affections, time, money, energies, children, and the like to these idolatrous *church* systems we are in!

THE VALIDATION

Jesus told a parable which sounds strangely like the story of Naboth because of the coveting, the murder, and the judgment contained in it.

"There was a certain householder, who planted a vineyard, hedged it round about, dug a winepress in it, built a tower, let it out to husbandmen, and went into a far country.

"When the time of the fruit drew near, he sent his servants to the husbandmen, that they might receive the fruits of it. And the husbandmen took his servants, and beat one, and killed another, and stoned another.

"Again, he sent other servants more than the first: and they did to them likewise. But last of all he sent unto them his son, saying, 'They will reverence my son.' But when the husbandmen saw the son, they said among themselves, 'This is the heir; come, let us kill him, and let us seize on his inheritance.' They caught him, cast him out of the vineyard, and slew him.

"When the lord therefore of the vineyard comes, what will he do to those husbandmen? "

They said to Him, "He will miserably destroy those wicked men, and will let out his vineyard to other husbandmen, which shall render him the fruits in their seasons."

Jesus said to them, "Did you never read in the scriptures, 'The stone which the builders rejected, the same is become the head of the corner: this is the Lord's doing, and it is marvelous in our eyes?' Therefore say I to you, the kingdom of God shall be taken from you, and given to a nation bringing forth the fruits thereof. And whosoever shall fall on this stone shall be broken: but on whomsoever it shall fall, it will grind him to powder."

And when the chief priests and Pharisees had heard his parables, they perceived that he spoke of them. But when they sought to lay hands on him, they feared the multitude, because they took him for a prophet. Matt. 21:33-46.

The householder in this parable is God, the Father. The vineyard is His assembly of called-out-ones, the true heirs of Abraham, heirs by faith. The husbandman was the nation of Israel, who by this time was ruled by the religious and political systems of the Pharisees, Sadducees, scribes, and rulers. The servants whom they killed were the prophets. The Son whom they also killed was Jesus Christ. The nation to whom He gave the care of the vineyard (the Kingdom of God) are the Gentiles.

This parable just as well speaks of the condition of the *church* system today, and the Nicolaitans in that *church* system today perpetuate the attitude of the Pharisees, Sadducees, scribes, and rulers. Once again, the Spirit of the Lord testifies that the vineyard (the called-out-ones) will be taken from them and given to those who will nurture the called-out-ones into the fullness of Christ. They will be shepherds who will seek nothing for themselves.

Ahab is a type of Self on the throne. Jezebel is the harlotry of seeking something for Self. When it comes to that Thing we call *church*, she connives to be on the throne—practicing her witchcraft to possess God's inheritance in the saints.

Chapter 13

Witchcraft in Everyday Life

*A*hab did an abominable thing in the sight of God: he married that woman Jezebel who brought her idolatries and witchcraft into the house of the Lord. Ahab's Jezebel, the Jezebel of Revelation 2:20, and the great whore of Revelation 18 were each known for their witchcraft.

As for Ahab's Jezebel, 2 Kings 9:22 tells us, "It came about, when Joram saw Jehu, that he said, 'Is it peace, Jehu?' And he answered, 'What peace, so long as the harlotries of your mother Jezebel and her witchcraft are so many?'"

As for "that woman Jezebel" in Revelation 2:20, Jesus said that she taught and seduced "...My servants to commit fornication, and to eat things sacrificed to idols." The Greek word for seduced has also been translated "beguiled" and "deceived." These terms are associated with witchcraft.

As for the great whore that sits on many waters, Revelation 18:23 mentions that all the nations were deceived by her sorcery.

WITCHCRAFT DEFINED

The practice of witchcraft is a deed of the flesh. Paul writes, "Now the works of the flesh are evident, which are: adultery, fornication, uncleanness, lewdness, idolatry, *sorcery*, hatred, contentions, jealousies, outbursts of wrath, selfish ambitions, dissensions, heresies, envy, murders, drunkenness, revelries, and the like; of which I tell you beforehand, just as I also told you in time past, that those who practice such things will not inherit the kingdom of God." Gal. 5:19-21 NKJV. The Greek word for sorcery is *pharmakeia* which refers to a person who prepares and uses magical remedies. The King James Version translates it "witchcraft".

While witchcraft is a deed of the flesh, the spirit of witchcraft can influence our flesh to do all the other deeds of the flesh. It can entice our flesh to commit adultery and fornication. It can manipulate circumstances in our relationships to stir up contentions, jealousies, and outbursts of wrath. It can control all aspects of our flesh to do evil if we allow it to take dominance.

Witchcraft, as a work of the flesh, has two dimensions to it. One is the strict, familiar concept that it ordinarily brings to mind. It conjures up the image of an old, bony-framed woman with a wrinkled face and a shrill voice, hunched over an iron kettle, brewing up a potion of spiders and herbs to cast spells on people. We think about voodoo dolls, ouija boards, tarot cards, crystal balls, palm reading, seances, astrology, meditation, parapsychology, psychic phenomena, and mental telepathy. The most blatant form of witchcraft is Satanic worship where children and animals are sacrificed for the sake of gaining spiritual power. All of these practices are the darker side of witchcraft. Jezebel certainly practiced the darker side of witchcraft and surrounded herself with prophets who did so. The Bible makes it absolutely clear that such practices are an abomination to God. Lev. 19:26; Deut. 18:10.

The other dimension of witchcraft, is broader and more subtle. I define it as *anything we do to manipulate other people to do things against their wills in order to achieve our own self-centered desires.* Manipulation is an attempt to control someone else. Control and manipulation are the practice of witchcraft. In our day we do not use witch's brew to control other people. Rather, we do such things as play on emotions, withhold affection, provoke fear, provoke guilt, intimidate with anger, lie and deceive, or use self-pity.

The practice of witchcraft in this broader sense of the term abounds in our lives and has devastating effects upon us in our everyday life. If we can see how it works in everyday life, perhaps we can see how widely it is practiced in this Thing we call *church.* (I will deal with the demons of witchcraft in the following chapter.)

THE WIDESPREAD EFFECTS OF WITCHCRAFT

The practice of witchcraft—trying to get others to do things against their wills—permeates every level of human experience, from politicians who deceive us to get our votes, to advertisers who send us subliminal messages, to merchants who try to hook us on their products, to clergy persons who try to dictate our consciences, to entertainers who play on our emotions. Everyone in the world wants something from us. They mostly want our money, and if they can, will exploit our bodies, souls, minds, time, and talents to get it. Most of us practice witchcraft without having an awareness of it. The practice of witchcraft is so subtle and common we either do not recognize it or have become de-sensitized to it. We just experience the frustration of it.

The practice of witchcraft is the principal cause of trouble in the world. It is the principle cause of trouble in the home between husbands and wives, parents and children, brothers and sisters who try to manipulate one another. It is the cause of strife between friends and nations. It is the major source of conflict in *churches*.

Guilt feelings, fear, depression, suspicion, mental ruminations and rehearsings, anger and bitterness, fantasies, confusion, jealousy, compulsions, and obsessions may be caused by the fleshly practice of witchcraft. Poverty, crime, sickness, disease, and conflicts in relationships are also among the effects of witchcraft.

Witchcraft influences those behaviors in our lives over which we are powerless—things to which we can be addicted: smoking, drinking, drugs, TV, the Internet, music, food, sports, pornography, sex, relationships, and gambling.

These effects of the practice of witchcraft are so universal that all of us will identify with at least some of these. Almost every one of us at some time or another will experience the frustration and anger that results from manipulation. The presence of witchcraft creates a negative atmosphere that drains life from everyone who is touched by it.

INDICATIONS OF WITCHCRAFT

Here are some of the indications of the subtle practices of witchcraft in everyday life:

Witchcraft is indicated by *lying* and *deceit*. Lying is lying whether we think of it as a big black lie or a little white lie. We differentiate between black and white lies to justify ourselves or to lessen the consequences. When we lie, we are hiding some truth in order to make something happen or to prevent a consequence from happening. Truth never has to be twisted, manipulated, forced, or in any way tampered with. Once it is tampered with, it is no longer truth. It has become a lie. God does not have to lie, connive, or contrive to get people to obey Him. He simply sets forth His Word in plain truth and commands that men obey.

Witchcraft is indicated by *self-strength*. We practice witchcraft when we put our trust in ourselves. We try to make things happen in our own strength, especially those things that should be left to the work of the Holy Spirit. Philippians 3:3 affirms that we as believers "are the circumcision who worship God in the spirit, and rejoice in Christ Jesus, and have no confidence in the flesh." Psalm 118:8 confirms: "It is better to trust in the Lord than to put confidence in man."

Witchcraft is indicated by one's attempt to unduly *control* his life and the lives of others. Insecure people try to make their worlds safer by building rigid structures for themselves and for others in their lives. When we are insecure, we think we need to control God, other people, our environment, and every circumstance of our lives. We attempt to control what we feel, think, say, and do.

Witchcraft is indicated by *fear, worry, doubt, anxiety,* and *restlessness.* When we are no longer able to control other people nor believe that we can trust God, we panic. However, we no longer need to fear, manipulate, and control other people and circumstances once we know who we are in Christ Jesus. We can "let go and let God...." We can rest in the knowledge that the Lord is God and is sovereign over all.

Witchcraft is indicated by *pride.* Pride is a form of lying because pride hides. It conceals the insecurity that prideful persons do not want others to see. Pride indicates an over-awareness and preoccupation with Self. It manifests itself in either self-exalted or self-abased egos. Self-abasement is false humility. It is pride in disguise.

Witchcraft is indicated by *rebellion.* It is the will of the flesh rising up against the will of God. King Saul came back from battle, having disobeyed God. God required Saul to utterly destroy the enemy. He did not do so. Instead, he brought some of the spoils of battle home with him. When questioned about it, he thought he could "con" God with the lame excuse that he had returned with the animals to make a sacrifice to God. The prophet Samuel answered, "Has the Lord as great delight in burnt offerings and sacrifices, as in obeying the voice of the Lord? Behold, to obey is better than sacrifice, and to hearken than the fat of rams. For *rebellion is as the sin of witchcraft,* and stubbornness is as iniquity and idolatry." 1 Sam. 15:22-23. Consequently, God rejected Saul from being King, not because he sinned—David sinned as much as Saul—but because of the condition of his heart. He was ambitious, deceitful, rebellious, stubborn, and idolatrous. Any ambition for Self is going to lead to the practice of witchcraft. Self will try to use people and coerce them to do things against their own wills.

Witchcraft is indicated by *stubbornness.* "Stubbornness is as iniquity and idolatry." 1 Sam. 15:23. Stubborn people are typically rigid, adamant, unreasonable, uncompromising, unyielding, and unteachable. They cannot concede to being wrong. They try to maintain their position and, thereby in this subtle way, practice witchcraft. People who have their confidence in God are not threatened by the suggestions, corrections, opinions, and actions of other people. They are able and willing to learn from others.

Witchcraft is indicated by *cursing.* Without realizing it, we often speak curses out of our mouths. We curse others, other things, and even ourselves. James 3:10 teaches us that our tongues bless God and, at the same time, curse men who are made in the image of God. "Out of the same mouth proceeds blessing and cursing. My brethren, these things ought not to be so." We pronounce curses when we speak *evil* words, *"cuss"* words, *false judgments, criticisms, or agree with an evil report.* Parents speak curses and practice witchcraft over their children when they call them "bad," "ugly," "stupid," "clumsy," or "no account." People, especially children, tend to become what we call them. I believe demons are assigned to try to make good on these curses.

Witchcraft is indicated by *talkativeness.* Talkative, rambling, interruptive persons are self-absorbed. Figuratively speaking, they have no ears. They dominate the conversation and often interrupt other people before others complete their thoughts. They are preoccupied with their own thoughts and are not really hearing what other people are saying. Consequently, they frequently misunderstand what other people are trying to say. They may use their talking to control and cling to others out of fear of losing them, even though their incessant talking has the reverse effect and drives listeners away. It is difficult to communicate with such persons. "Talkative people also use their wall of words to isolate themselves from real intimacy," observes Valerie McCarley.

Witchcraft is indicated by *unforgiveness.* We practice witchcraft when we deliberately withhold forgiveness from others in order to manipulate their feelings or actions. We think we are punishing them by withholding forgiveness, but we are mostly punishing ourselves. We can be held hostage by our own unforgiveness of others and by the unforgiveness of others toward us. Ultimately, however, we who refuse to forgive become entangled in the root of bitterness. Bitterness can kill us.

Witchcraft is indicated by *impatience.* Impatience means we are in a hurry for something to happen. We rush through traffic, get angry at people who get in our way or slow us down, and make impulsive decisions to buy things we do not need. We get impatient with circumstances, other people, ourselves, and God. "Why doesn't He do this or that?" Impatience is pushing for something for Self in disregard for others or for God's timing and will.

Witchcraft is indicated by *distrust* in God. That is what motivates us to resort to it. It disregards the reality of the lordship of Jesus Christ. When we surrender to His lordship, we enter into a trust relationship with God. We trust that He is absolutely sovereign and that the Holy Spirit is our competent guide. We are secure in knowing who we are in Christ. No one can put fear, guilt, or condemnation upon us, nor can they provoke us to anger. We seek God's will only and not something for Self (which is usually at the expense of others). We will passionately determine to keep other people free of our control and manipulations. When we learn faith in God—that He is sovereign and in control—we come into that promised rest of Hebrews 4:1-11.

The practice of witchcraft is further indicated by *domination, intimidation, acts of violence, nagging, contriving, strife, stress, sulking, whining, charm, flattery, seduction, rape, blackmail, bribery, entrapment, jealousy, hypochondria, mind control, rejection* and the *threat of rejection,* the *power of suggestion, subliminal advertising, game-playing,* and *competitiveness.* The practices of witchcraft as related to *church* are addressed in the next chapter.

INDICATIONS OF THE HOLY SPIRIT

In contrast to witchcraft, the Holy Spirit is indicated by the power of God at work in our lives. He produces honesty, truthfulness, straightforwardness, trust, faith, confidence, rest, peace, joy, life, blessings, righteousness, light, power, health and healing, humility, submission, a quiet and gentle spirit, forgiveness, freedom, and liberty.

The Holy Spirit operates when we base our security and faith in Jesus Christ as Lord. Zechariah 4:6b reads, "...not by might, nor by power, but by My Spirit, says the Lord of hosts." A life in the Spirit walks in the confidence of Psalms 37:23: "The steps of a good [righteous] man are ordered by the Lord."

James 3:14-18 summarizes this contrast between the Holy Spirit and witchcraft for us: "But if you have bitter envying and strife in your hearts, glory not, and lie not against the truth. This wisdom descends not from above, but is earthly, sensual, devilish. For where envying and strife is, there is confusion and every evil work. But the wisdom that is from above is first pure, then peaceable, gentle, and easy to be entreated, full of mercy and good fruits, without partiality, and without hypocrisy. And the fruit of righteousness is sown in peace by those who make peace." Note that James used these three words: earthly, sensual, and devilish. These agree with the progression of thought presented here that the flesh (that which is *earthly)* seeks something for Self (that which is *sensual)* which invites the demonic (that which is *devilish).*

Witchcraft is a negative and destructive force of the human flesh and will. Any form or degree of witchcraft is an abomination to God. It is a counterfeit to the Holy Spirit. God's life-giving Holy

Spirit will not abide where witchcraft is practiced.

Just as we practice witchcraft in everyday life, we can be sure that it is also being practiced in the *churches*.

Chapter 14

Witchcraft in the Church

*W*hat could the practice of witchcraft possibly have to do with the *church*? Much in many different ways. William's experience is one example.

William had been called by the *church* officials to pastor their little independent fellowship. After much prayer and consultation, he and his wife agreed. They left their home community to face the challenges of this new work. He tells about it this way:

> I knew from the beginning that Stella was in control of this *church*, I guess I ignored the red flags. This little group of people had unanimously decided it was God's will for me to be their pastor and after much prayer, I accepted. It was deceiving at first, because my initial contacts were with her husband and another man. Then it happened. One incident after another. She came against everything I did. She resisted my preaching. She controlled the finances and the Christian school the *church* ran. She did it all through her husband. He was her voice.
>
> Then the *church* officials called a meeting with me. I could tell something was wrong when I walked in. They said they wanted me to be at the *church* every morning by six o'clock to handle the daycare when the children came in.
>
> "I thought you wanted me to pastor the *church*—to spend time in prayer, study, and ministry. The daycare was never mentioned," I replied.
>
> They answered back, "There's not any men down here. We need somebody down here if light bulbs need to be changed."
>
> "Wait a minute," I said, "I didn't come here to change light bulbs." I knew then they didn't want me around anymore. So I asked them if they believed God had sent me here. I challenged them to think about it before they answered. I asked each one in turn and they each replied, "No." "Then we don't need to carry this meeting on any further," I told them.

Stella's husband said, "Well I'm sure we can work out something."

"Brother," I answered, "you just told me that you didn't think God sent me here. If you don't think God sent me here, then why would you want to work things out?" This was the demise of that relationship. We were fired just one month after we had moved on the field.

Stella wanted William to pastor her *church* as long as she could control and manipulate him to do what she wanted done. Trouble broke out between them, however, anytime he did anything or said anything that threatened her hold on things.

She operated in the Jezebel spirit and her husband perfectly played out the Ahab role. When they brought their manipulations and control issues into the life and affairs of the *church*, they practiced witchcraft in the *church*—witchcraft being: *anything we do to manipulate other people to do things against their wills in order to achieve our own self-centered desires.* Wherever it is practiced, or however slightly it is practiced, witchcraft is still witchcraft.

WITCHCRAFT IN THE *CHURCH*

People practice witchcraft in the *church* as thoughtlessly as they do in everyday life. It is an abomination to God when it is practiced in any arena, but more especially when we practice it among one another in the family of God.

Jesus is the head of His body, the called-out-ones. The Holy Spirit is His administrator. Those who follow Jesus are obedient to His Holy Spirit. The Holy Spirit establishes the Kingdom of God. It can never be established by the hand of self-strength and the practice of witchcraft.

When men assume headship over Christ's body and people submit to that false headship, the flesh rather than the Spirit of Jesus is operating. The fact that such terms as ambition, impatience, competition, success, promotion, contention, contrariness, argumentativeness, divisiveness, and unyieldedness are commonplace among those who rule the *churches* and abide in them is evidence enough that they are operating in the flesh.

The flesh nature of man is controlling and manipulative—thus, it engages in the practice of witchcraft. When what you have is headed by man (or woman), it will always be under the rule of witchcraft—men building their own kingdoms under the pretext of being the Kingdom of God.

The structures of denominations and institutionalized *churches* are headed by man; therefore, they are out of scriptural order. Those who rule the *churches* may say that Christ is the head of their *church*, but He is not. He cannot be the head of many different bodies. He is the head of His body. There is only one body of Christ. If Jesus were in charge of these man-ruled organizations, there would be no need for men and women to politic for positions. If He were the head of the *churches*, there would only be one church because there is only one body of Christ. On the contrary, the *churches* are divided one against the other.

It is an alarming thing to realize that this Thing we call *church* is not ruled by the Holy Spirit, but by witchcraft. In the street-savvy words of Bob Hughey, "Everything that is called Christian and Holy Spirit, ain't. Be warned."

SELF-AGGRANDIZEMENT

Self-seeking people who rule the *churches* are typically fueled by the need to increase themselves in power, position, riches, and domination. They are Nicolaitans who are prodded by the Jezebel spirit.

They garner large sums of unrighteously gained tithes and offerings to build elaborate edifices for themselves rather than beautifying the Lord of glory and His bride. They seduce others to join them rather than joining others to Jesus Christ. They devise schemes, programs, and marketing plans complete with logos and slogans to entice people to join them. They inspire loyalty and commitment to themselves and their vision rather than to Jesus and His vision for the bride.

They bind people to their own laws and phony doctrines. They guilt-provoke people to sign pledge cards, causing them to make oaths that God has not asked them to make. They build their identities around their names, positions, clerical collars, titles, denominations, traditions, doctrines, and heritage. They deceive people into thinking that busyness is godliness. They use their power to endow other people with power, that they might ally those other people to themselves. They give the more honored seats to the persons who come in wearing the gold rings and costly apparel. James 2:2. People, their money, and their talents are rungs on the ladder they use to climb to the heights of their own ambitions which are fueled by their imaginations.

PERSONAL HIDDEN AGENDA

Self-seeking people who rule the *churches* have personal agendas. Self-seeking personal agendas conflict with God's agenda.

Their agendas are often hidden. Different people have different agendas. Bishop Pete built a new sanctuary out of his need for identity. Father David entered the ministry to please his dad. Reverend Dan earned a doctoral degree to receive recognition and better positions. Dr. Anthony was committed to writing a new book every year just to maintain his popularity.

People with hidden agendas need supporters to carry out their plans. They may want increased *church* memberships, newer and bigger buildings, inflated reputations, or better salaries. They need noses and nickels to achieve their desired high standings. They know that "bigness" impresses people. They have taught each other that. So the bigger they get, the more impressive they think they will become. The more popular many ministers become, the more riches people lavish upon them.

Their agendas must be kept hidden from their supporters, for the truth would result in a loss of support; therefore, they seek to gain loyalty and support by provoking fear, condemnation, guilt, emotionalism, and by falsifying reports.

APPEALS FOR MONEY

Self-seeking people who rule the *churches* depend upon other people to make themselves and their *churches* successful. Naive and unsuspecting "partners" or members are deceived into believing that giving to these ministries or *churches* ruled by people with personal agendas are "as unto the Lord." These ministries often make people feel guilty if they do not give as much as they might freely choose to give. They extract tithes and offerings from their constituency, deceiving them into believing that they are "seeding" into the Kingdom of God when, in fact, they are empowering the kingdoms of men.

They appeal to their supporters' emotions in order to persuade them to give to their ministry or *church*. If they are TV personalities, they may promise to send their supporters a free gift for their donation: books, tapes, prayer cloths, anointing oil from Israel, or some other token. Their mail-outs are carefully, professionally designed to tug on the heartstrings of donors, manipulating them into giving money.

They falsely teach that their *churches* are the storehouses for those members who "belong" to them. Many of them accumulate wealth and lavish it back upon themselves in the building, maintenance, and preservation of their organizations and institutions while the poor around the world go without food, clothing, shelter, and the gospel of the Kingdom of God. Jesus never even slightly suggested that, "Inasmuch as you build your buildings and preserve your institutions, you have done it unto Me." Rather He said that inasmuch as we feed the hungry, give a drink to a stranger, clothe the naked, visit the sick and imprisoned, we are doing these things to Him. Matt. 25:35-40.

ANGER AND RAGE

Some of those self-seeking people who rule the *churches* may be insecure control addicts who need to maintain a sense of order in their lives to feel safe. They may be perfectionists who impose their standard of perfection upon others. When others fail to meet their standards, they become frustrated and rageful. Rage is part of their arsenal of weapons to manipulate others into conformity. Pastor Daniel was such a one.

Pastor Daniel's *church*—and I emphasize that it was "his" *church*—served as a showcase for his drive to perform. He was an accomplished orator, avid reader, and had a winning personality. His setting was exquisite and his staging was professional. He attracted crowds and multiplied members, but he could not keep them. "Why do people go out the back door as quickly as they come in the front?" he asked.

He did not want to hear the truth. He wanted it to be "their" fault, not his. People left because of his misuse of authority. He was spiritually and emotionally abusive. It was, after all, "his" *church* and no one was permitted to do anything unless invited to do so. His *church* was his theater, his pulpit was his stage, and he was the show. Those who had the slightest thought of contradicting him, especially if they had been given a place of leadership, became suspect. They had to be dealt with, usually tongue-lashed.

Leaving his *church* was not a pleasant option. Those who tried were often threatened by the suggestion that they would be out of God's will and bad things would happen to them. The loyalty of many within his membership was based on fear and intimidation.

His Jezebel wife fueled his feverish manipulations with her own. She ruled surreptitiously behind his throne. Most everyone knew that, but no one dared to speak a word. "Hush" was the operative rule in this extended dysfunctional family he called a *church*.

FLATTERY

Self-seeking people who rule the *churches* often flatter their prospects in order to win them in. "You two have so much to offer. It's a shame you aren't involved in a *church* somewhere." That one has been used on my wife and me a few times. We were said to be the poster couple for one *church* we attended. I think it was meant to flatter us, but it did not.

Flattery is enticing, seductive, and deceitful. When we fail to see what is happening to us, we are taken in by it. It has the deceitful motive of complimenting us in order to win favor from us. A true compliment does not have an ulterior motive, but those who flatter are putting on the charm in order to get something from us for themselves. They are like the adulterous woman in Proverbs 7:4-5 who preys upon believers who lack discernment: "Say to wisdom, You are my sister; and call understanding your kinswoman: that they may keep you from the strange [adulterous] woman, from the stranger who flatters with her words."

Flattery is an appeal to the flesh for greatness, grandeur, sensual pleasure, success, and riches—all having to do with things in the world.

POSSESSIVENESS AND OWNERSHIP

Self-seeking people who rule the *churches* are typically possessive and claim ownership over their constituency. If they own you, they can control you. If they cannot control you, they will disown you.

Membership in the *churches* is a claim of ownership that the *churches* have over a set number of people. All *churches* and denominations do it. Pick any. In 1997, the Southern Baptist Convention reported 15,891,514 members and 40,887 churches.[22] Why do we need to know how many people *belong to us?* Why do we need to know how many people were in Sunday School and worship services? Why is it important to compare this figure with "this time last year"? Who are we counting for? We count because we measure our success with numbers.

I was in a meeting as a new believer and decided to count the attendance. A still, small voice in my spirit interrupted and said, "Don't count. You don't know who counts." I found out in time, as people came and went, how right that was. Besides, are we not counting the tares along with the wheat? Jesus told us that the wheat and the tares grow up together. Matt. 13:24-30. We do not always know who they are. If we need to count noses and know that we are including tares in that number, then we need to know that we are not counting as God counts. We are counting something for Self.

---

[22]*World Magazine*, 30 May 1998, 17.

Perhaps we count to determine how strong we are. The Bible records three times when a census was taken of Israel. The first two times, God ordered it. God commanded Moses to take a census of all the congregation of the children of Israel from twenty years and older, numbering their armies. Num. 1. The second time, the LORD told Moses and Eleazar to take the sum (census) of "all the congregation of the children of Israel, from twenty years old and upward, throughout their fathers' house, all that are able to go to war in Israel." Num. 26.

The third time is when King David ordered a census on his own. 1 Chronicles 21 tells how Satan stood up against Israel and provoked David to number Israel. 2 Samuel 24:1 reports this story saying, "the anger of the LORD was kindled against Israel, and He moved David against them to say, 'Go, number Israel and Judah.'" The key to what is going on here is found in verse two of both passages. David ordered the census saying, "that *I* may know the number of people." God was greatly displeased with David and sent a plague upon Israel killing seventy thousand men. David's desire to count his increase resulted in great losses. He put his confidence in the strength of numbers, rather than in God. It was good for God to count Israel. Israel belonged to Him. It was not good for David to count Israel. Israel did not belong to him. David sought ownership of the citizenry for himself. It was something Satan put in his heart to do.

We are fascinated by numbers. We build our significance upon how big we perceive ourselves to be. Size is a matter of opinion. In order to determine how big we are, we have to compare ourselves with others. Comparing ourselves with others is a prideful and competitive spirit which has no place in the Kingdom of God. *Church* rulers relate to "their" *church* members as extensions of themselves. They validate themselves by their statistics. They feel they must possess people in order to keep them.

Sonny was at the ball park with his kids one steamy, summer night and saw Pastor Gene. Sonny asked, "Do you have someone here?" "All of mine are here," he answered. Sonny was puzzled by his answer. Sonny knew Pastor Gene did not have children of his own playing ball that night. Pastor Gene explained, "If they are a member of my *church*, they belong to me." Sonny regretted later that he had not asked him at the time, "Do you really want that responsibility? They are not your sheep. They belong to Jesus."

Taking possession and claiming ownership of God's sheep is a very grievous thing to God.

HYPE

Self-seeking people who rule the *churches* often hype things up to make themselves look good. Hype in this context is trying to make the Holy Spirit "happen" in self-strength. Hype is what leaders do to pretend the presence of God. These leaders have to make their services look like God is moving in their midst whether He is or not. He is not, so they substitute hype for Spirit. They try to make things happen that are not happening, or try to make it look like things are happening when they are not.

Hype is the practice of witchcraft. We see and hear it in many "charismatic" *church* services, conferences, and meetings when the praise and worship leader prolongs the energized music for an hour or so, pretending that the Holy Spirit is present or hoping to invoke His presence. When the Holy Spirit chooses not to manifest Himself, the congregation may be brow-beaten for not singing loud enough, clapping their hands long enough, praying hard enough, or dancing in the Spirit wildly enough. "Put your hands together and give the Lord a clap offering." "Somebody give me an amen!" We are manipulated to do and say things that we do not want to do and say—things that are not in our hearts to do and say. We fake it anyway because we do not want to stand out in the crowd, to be thought of as rebellious, or to be accused of quenching the Spirit. When we fake something, that makes us a fake—Pharisees.

Those who practice hype, such as we often witness on so-called "Christian TV", falsely measure the Holy Spirit's presence by the loudness of the music, the emotional fervor of the audience, the fancy footwork of the preacher, the religious prompting of amens from the crowd, or the number of persons slain in the Spirit—"doing carpet time" as they say. Some ministries look to these things to validate themselves.

PERFORMANCE MENTALITY

Many self-seeking people who rule the *churches* have turned their *churches* and ministries into entertainment centers and seek ministers who are crowd-pleasing showmen. Their theater-designed *church* auditoriums and "entertain-me" hungry congregations demand this performance mentality.

"Christian" entertainment is big business today. The self-seeking, secular-owned executives within the so-called "Christian" music industry are driven by the corporate bottom line. If that which we call "Christian" can become an industry, it is not the real thing. Christian "artists" (the big ones are called "stars") are the product of this profit-driven industry and are themselves often

Chapter 15

Legalism

*T*hose who rule the *churches* are typically legalistic.

Technically, legalism is the literal, strict, and excessive conformity to a law or religious order. Bob Hughey says, "Legalism is the system by which we do things to try to get to God." *It is putting confidence in the flesh in an attempt to find acceptance with God.*

Paul wrote the Philippian believers regarding this and told them to beware of the circumcision party [also called Judaizers] who taught that "unless you are circumcised after the manner of Moses, you cannot be saved." Acts 15:1. They made circumcision a precondition to being a Christian. Paul clarified the issue with the Galatians saying, "We are the circumcision, who worship God in the Spirit, rejoice in Christ Jesus, and *have no confidence in the flesh.*" Phil. 3:2-3. The circumcision party was putting confidence in the flesh to find acceptance with God.

We can be thankful for this controversy Paul had with the Judaizers because it inspired him to draw a clear line of difference between grace and legalism. Unfortunately, though, those who put confidence in the flesh are still very much among us. For the most part they rule the *churches*. Thus, this line between grace and legalism still needs to be drawn.

Of all the deceptions perpetuated in the *church* system, legalism is the most frightening because it looks so right, but is so terribly wrong. The works of the law—or in present-day terms, *church* laws and *church* work—are presented as "the way" to salvation rather than the work of God's grace through Christ Jesus. These works become substitutes for Jesus.

LEGALISM REQUIRES SOMETHING MORE

Legalistic people require more of us than God has required. We live near some Mennonites. Though their houses are scattered throughout the larger community, they are a community to themselves. They wear distinctive clothes, live by certain codes, and worship together in a church building they have named after themselves. I greatly respect these people. The simplicity and modesty of their lifestyle is something to be desired. Yet I must ask, "Do I have to be a Mennonite in order to be a Christian?" If not, then why would I want to become one? Isn't being a baptized believer in Jesus Christ enough? Peter said to those present on the day of Pentecost, "Repent, and be baptized every one of you in the name of Jesus Christ for the remission of sins, and you shall receive the gift of the Holy Ghost." Acts 2:38. No other requirement was put upon them to have what the twelve had. If I cannot be a Christian without being a Mennonite, then what must I do to be a Mennonite? Do I have to wear the clothes, behave the code, attend every meeting? At what point am I considered a full-fledged Mennonite?

From observation, it would appear that I would have to do more to be a Mennonite than to be a Roman Catholic, Episcopalian, Lutheran, Methodist, Presbyterian, Baptist, Pentecostal, charismatic, member of the Church of Christ, or some independent *church*. Yet, in each of these groups, I still have to "do" something in addition to believing in Jesus in order to be one of these—at the very least, I would have to join their *church*. I would be expected to join something Jesus never required me to join, something that did not even exist in New Testament days—*church*. So, what is it they want me to join? Is this not the circumcision party in disguise?

LEGALISM IS THE OUTWARD DOING OF THINGS

Legalistic people are those who concentrate on the outward doing of things to attain favor with God. Any attempt to *earn* our salvation is called works-righteousness. However, Paul wrote the Roman believers asserting that no flesh can be justified by the deeds [works] of the law. Rather, we are justified freely by the grace of Jesus Christ through the redemption that is in Him. Therefore, Paul concluded that a man is justified by faith without the deeds of the law. Rom. 3:20, 24, 28.

Legalism is based on performance. It implies that we are rewarded for what we do and are chastised for what we do not do. It is based on works. This is precisely why the *churches* are dead. Paul wrote, "Christ is become of no effect unto you, whosoever of you are justified by the law; you are fallen from grace." Gal. 5:4. Whenever we go back under law, whether it is Old Testament law or modern day *church* law, we fall from grace.

Law is doing. Grace is *being*. Law has to do with what we "should" do, but cannot. Grace has to do with what God has already done for us. (We call a people to be like Mary, to sit at the feet of Jesus, but we love to have the Marthas around. Most of the activities in the *churches* depend upon the Marthas. Luke 10:38-42.)

If I try to legislate what you must do to act like a good Christian, then I am under the law and putting you under the law. If, on the other hand, I introduce you to Jesus, who is the perfect law of God, and He legislates His law from within you by changing your nature, then I bring you to the grace of God. Grace is the power of God at work within you to perform His word within you. Faith actively pursues the grace of God. Faith will never pursue law.

The writer of Hebrews told how the Israelites failed to enter into God's promised rest. If God promised it, then there must be a people who will enter into it. His promised rest is rest from dead works. "For he who has entered His rest has himself also ceased from his works as God did from His." Heb 4:10.

LEGALISM ATTEMPTS TO PERFECT BY THE FLESH

Legalistic people are those who attempt to perfect themselves and one another by the flesh. Paul wrote, "O foolish Galatians...This only would I learn of you, did you receive the Spirit by the works of the law, or by the hearing of faith? Are you so foolish? having begun in the Spirit, are you now made perfect by the flesh?" Gal. 3:1-3.

We think we know what God expects of us mentally, physically, spiritually, and morally, and we try to legislate that in our own and one another's lives. We invent codes of dress and behavior that we think exemplify holiness. Unless a change of nature has taken place on the inside of us, however, the changes on the outside are in vain. We are phony. The inside of us always has a way of shining through that thin, transparent, gilded exterior we exhibit to others.

God is the only one who can change us on the inside. Ezek. 36:25-27. He made a promise to Israel through Jeremiah: "This is the covenant that I will make with the house of Israel after that time," declares the Lord. "I will put My law in their minds and write it on their hearts. I will be their God, and they will be My people." Jer. 31:33. This was accomplished by Jesus Christ who was and is the "word made flesh." John 1:14. That word of God is engrafted in all who believe in the name of the Lord Jesus Christ. "Receive with meekness the engrafted [implanted] word, which is able to save your souls." James 1:21.

The law of God has been deposited within our human spirits and we have been transformed by it. Therefore, we no longer live according to the outward working of the law, but by the inward working of God's law. That's grace!

LEGALISM IS DIVISIVE

Legalistic people tend to be divisive. They may not intend to be divisive, but their legalistic ways cause division. The more legalistic they are, the more they tend to splinter over little, non-essential things.

I was told the story of two sectarian Christian groups, living in distant communities from each other, who tried to work out a plan for their young people to marry outside of their home communities. The leaders of these two groups were unable to come into agreement with such a plan because of a religious issue. One group believed that the men should have five pins on their coats and the other group believed in only four.

Two Churches of Christ exist in a small Tennessee town where, according to their own doctrine, only one should have existed. One group believed it was okay to have a kitchen in their church building and the other did not. So they split.

Silly and petty rules in the *churches* often cause divisions and deep hurts which sometimes lead to rejection of individuals by their own families. *Churches* of every kind have divided over nonessential issues. *Churches* by their very nature are programmed to splinter.

Paul explained to the Corinthians, "We being many are one bread, and one body: for we are all partakers of that one bread." 1 Cor. 10:17. Later he wrote, "For as the body is one, and has many members, and all the members of that one body, being many, are one body: so also is Christ. For by one Spirit are we all baptized into one body, whether we be Jews or Gentiles, whether we be bond or free; and have been all made to drink into one Spirit...But now are they many members, yet one body...That there should be no schism in the body; but that the members should have the same care one for another." 1 Cor. 12:12-13, 20, 25.

Paul appealed to the Ephesians to forebear one another in all lowliness, meekness, long-suffering, love, endeavoring to keep the unity of the Spirit in the bond of peace because of one inescapable truth: "There is one body, and one Spirit, even as you are called in one hope of your calling, one Lord, one faith, one baptism, one God and Father of all, who is above all, and through all, and in you all." Eph. 4: 2-6.

There is only one body. This one body of Christ is not and cannot be many bodies. Therefore, if that which you are in can be divided, it is not the real thing.

LEGALISM LEADS TO ISOLATIONISM

Legalistic leaders in extreme situations tend to isolate themselves and those who follow after them. Fear controls their behavior. These leaders fear that those under their influence might leave them. The more protective they feel they have to be, the more restrictive they become. They restrict the questions their followers are allowed to ask, the people they are allowed to know, the literature they are allowed to read, and the things they are allowed to listen to. They must protect those under their thumb from outside influences that would cause them to doubt—or worse yet, leave the fold. Violators are made to feel blasphemous.

We are to be holy, sanctified. Holiness and sanctification are from the same Greek word that means separation. Hebrews 12:14 reads, "Follow peace with all men, and *holiness*, without which no man shall see the Lord." We are to separate ourselves from sin and the world unto God, but this kind of separation is not isolation. We are to be *in* the world as light and salt, but not *of* the world. We cannot be the body of Christ in isolation. We are a body, His body, sent to accomplish His work in the world. We cannot accomplish His work as His body if we isolate one from the other. In spite of modern ecumenism (*churches* attempting cooperation while maintaining their differences), *churches* by their very nature cut themselves off one from the other.

LEGALISM IS EMPTY, MECHANICAL RITUAL

Legalistic people do works out of a joyless sense of duty, thinking that God will be pleased with their performance or that He might grant them "merited" favor. It is empty ritual.

So it is with foot washing. Some traditions believe that foot washing is an ordinance like water baptism and the Lord's supper. They may set aside arbitrary times once a month, every three months, or once a year to wash one another's feet. When the Holy Spirit leads someone to wash another's feet, it can prove to be powerful and meaningful and usually conveys a message of spiritual significance; but to impose foot washing as a requirement for being saved, for being right, or for being spiritual is to turn it into legalistic dead works. The same can be said for any act of worship or service. When things are done mechanically, they are generally meaningless works of the flesh.

The scribes and Pharisees were quite given to mechanical, ritualistic observation of days, and seasons, and laws—most of which were outgrowths of their own traditions. In one of His many scathing remarks to them, Jesus quoted Isaiah saying, "This people draws near unto Me with their mouth, and honors Me with their lips; but their hearts are far from Me. But in vain they do worship me, teaching for doctrines the commandments of men." Matt. 15:8-9.

LEGALISM IS JUDGMENTAL

Legalistic people tend to make critical judgments against other people. Perhaps you know Bob, or Jane, or Suzy, or Tom. By any other name, they are the same. They are those who have forgotten who they were before they were converted. They have forgotten that they, too, were once lost, rebellious, stubborn, self-centered, and self-willed persons of flesh and sin. Some never knew that they were lost, rebellious, stubborn, self-centered, and self-willed. They who once needed compassion and mercy lack compassion and mercy for others. They "got saved" and for some strange reason hardened their hearts toward others who are not yet saved. In severe cases, they will have nothing to do with "the sinner" or with anyone whose belief system is different from theirs. Judgmental persons make critical evaluations of others and want to impose their idea of righteousness on others.

What we judge is different from *how* we judge. If we judge with malice and contempt in our hearts, we become judgmental and thereby enter into sin. Judgmentalism judges others out of the intolerance of one's flesh. It ministers condemnation to those who are judged. We forget that we shall all be judged by the Lord one day. "But why do you judge your brother? or why do you set at nought your brother? for we shall all stand before the judgment seat of Christ." Rom. 14:10. It is one thing to call a brother to repentance out of love and compassion for his soul and quite another to assign him to hell with contempt in our hearts. We must be careful therefore *how* we judge.

This entire book is a judgment against that, Thing we call *church*. We are to discern what God is saying. We then speak those God-given revelations, visions, dreams, and understandings given to us in order, if need be, to call one another to repentance. We call sin, sin. We judge what God judges, but when we bring our own agendas, opinions, or feelings into the situation, we turn righteous judging into critical, legalistic judgmentalism.

As for this harlot system of men's traditions we call *church*, it has already been judged by God. Revelation 17:1 reads, "And there came one of the seven angels which had the seven vials, and talked with me, saying unto me, Come here; I will show unto you the *judgment* of the great whore that sits upon many waters." And Revelation 18:10: "Standing afar off for the fear of her torment, saying, Alas, alas, that great city Babylon, that mighty city! for in one hour is your *judgment* come." I am compelled by the Holy Spirit of God to "show the house to the house..." not to sit in judgment of others, but to call to repentance those whose hearts are given to their idolatries rather than to the Lord.

LEGALISM IS BONDAGE

Legalistic people put others in bondage to their works. Paul exhorted the Galatians, "Stand fast therefore in the liberty wherewith Christ has made us free, and be not entangled again with the yoke of bondage." Gal. 5:1.

Legalism puts us in bondage to the law itself. Grace gives us the power of God within to obey the Law-giver. James Ryle has essentially defined grace as the empowering presence of God that enables us to be what He has called us to be and to do what He has called us to do in Christ. The essence of grace requires that our relationship with God and our works of obedience be based upon what God has done and not upon what we could ever do.

Though the bride of Christ has been set free by the grace of God, she is, for the most part, still in the *churches* and is held captive by *church* laws. When we are in the flesh, in unbelief, under law, or into doing works that God has not ordained, we will be in bondage to these things—flesh, unbelief, law, and works. When we are in the Spirit, in faith, in grace, and in rest, we will be free of these things—flesh, unbelief, law, and works.

The bondage of legalism occurs when our laws, rules, and regulations put God in a box and then we try to fit everyone else into those same boxes. If they do not fit into the box, they are considered outsiders and even infidels.

LEGALISM CONDEMNS US

Legalistic people put others under condemnation. When we are put under man-made laws that we are not able to fulfill, we feel guilty, ashamed, and condemned. The law condemns us. Paul wrote, "For by the law is the knowledge of sin." Rom. 3:20.

Grace, on the other hand, acquits us. The law of God tells us what is required of us, but has no power to make us obedient. Grace is that power of God. The law condemns; grace empowers. Romans 8:1 reads, "There is therefore now no condemnation to those who are in Christ Jesus, who walk not after the flesh, but after the Spirit."

The Lord dealt with Larry about using doctors. Larry had come to a place of confidence in the Lord that all things were under His control. It was no longer a question of healing with Larry; it was a question of God's will being done. Larry had faith. It was not his faith, but the Lord's faith in him to endure whatever sickness and infirmity that came upon him without subjecting himself to medical treatment. Larry was careful not to make this a rule for everyone. Had He said, "The Lord has shown me it is wrong to go to doctors and therefore it is wrong for anyone to go doctors," he would have moved from grace to legalism. If we make going to doctors or not going to doctors a rule for everyone, we are legalistic. Those laws soon become impossible requirements for salvation.

LEGALISM IS FEAR-BASED

Legalistic people motivate with fear. Terrible consequences are implied if we fail to abide by those laws.

"I was born, baptized, and received instruction in the Catholic Church," Lillie said. "All of us were taught to follow the directions of the priests. We received the sacraments frequently, Holy Communion and Confession. At that time the Catholic church did not encourage its members to read the Bible. That was left to the priests. It wasn't until I was married and had five children that I felt a hunger to know God in a more personal way. I couldn't tell you anything about the Old or New Testament. My husband and I started attending a non-denominational church where they taught about the Bible. I truly sensed the presence of the Holy Spirit there. Yet, I could not break away from the hold the Catholic Church had on me. We would go to mass early on Sunday, then slip away to this other church afterwards. We did this for about three years. The fear of not receiving the Eucharist and losing its graces, possibly losing our salvation, kept us tied to the Catholic church. Slowly, we were delivered from that fear as we received more understanding from the scriptures."

Paul wrote, "For you have not received the spirit of bondage again to fear; but you have received the Spirit of adoption, whereby we cry, Abba, Father." Rom. 8:15. "For God has not given us the spirit of fear; but of power, and of love, and of a sound mind." 2 Tim. 1:7. We are to fear God; not men nor the made-up religious laws, rules, and regulations imposed by men.

LEGALISM KILLS US

Legalistic people deprive others of the life of God with their works. Paul wrote the Corinthians explaining, God "also has made us able ministers of the new testament; not of the letter, but of the spirit: for the letter kills, but the spirit gives life." 2 Cor. 3:6.

The Galatians were still observing religious days, months, seasons, and years over which Paul anguished, "I am afraid for you, lest I have labored for you in vain." Gal. 4:8-11 NKJV.

Most Christians are bound by what their *church* system says is proper Christian practice. In some traditions, individuals have little to say about how they dress, where they go, what they do, what they believe, and how they are to behave. These things are dictated to them, and they do them by rote. They rarely know why these things are required of them. *Church* systems have no life to give. Moreover, they quench the Spirit with their carnal meetings, formalities, traditions, rituals, dogmas, rules, programs, and regulations.

We tend to make religious laws and systems out of the truths of God and follow them instead of following God. The Kingdom of God has to do with the living reality of Jesus Christ and the power of His Holy Spirit who is at work within us to bring about God's ultimate intentions. Jesus could never be squeezed into the systems and formulas we concoct out of our carnal minds. Watch out for them! They are killers.

Those who gather only in the name of Jesus as appointed by the Holy Spirit are more likely to express the spontaneous life of Jesus in their midst. When the Spirit of Jesus is present, so will be the fruit of the Holy Spirit. The bride of Christ is characterized by liberty, love, praise, the word, fruit, ministry, gifts of the Holy Spirit, fellowship, blessing, edification, and service.

LEGALISM IS A CURSE

Legalistic people put others under the curse of the law. Paul stated, "For as many as are of the works of the law are under the curse: for it is written, Cursed is every one who continues not in all things which are written in the book of the law to do them." Gal. 3:10. The law was given to show us the perfect will of God. We are required to keep the whole law of God if we are to be righteous in the sight of God. Since it is impossible for us to keep the whole law, it becomes a curse to us. Rather than giving life, it kills us. Rom. 7:7. Paul argues that the more we try to obey the law outwardly in the flesh, the more we are bound to do the very thing we do not wish to do. Rom. 7:21.

At best, the laws that are put on us by religious people in the *church* systems can only be observed outwardly. No change of nature has taken place. Therefore, any requirement for us to adhere to a belief system, join and regularly attend *church*, dress a certain way, perform certain rituals, or abide by certain laws, rules, and regulations puts us under a curse. We are trying to make ourselves righteous by laws we cannot keep in our hearts.

Those who impose the law upon others not only put a curse

upon others, but are themselves accursed. Paul warned the Galatians that if "we, or an angel from heaven, preach any other gospel unto you than that which we have preached unto you, let him be accursed." Gal. 1:8. He meant business and repeated himself. "As we said before, so say I now again, if any man preach any other gospel unto you than that you have received, let him be accursed." Gal. 1:9.

Thank God "Christ has redeemed us from the curse of the law, being made a curse for us: for it is written, Cursed is every one who hangs on a tree." Gal. 3:13. Grace blesses.

LEGALISM IS BEWITCHING

Legalistic people bewitch others by persuasion and intimidation. Paul exhorted, "O foolish Galatians, who has bewitched you, that you should not obey the truth, before whose eyes Jesus Christ has been evidently set forth, crucified among you?" Gal. 3:1. It was as though a spell had been cast upon the Galatians by the circumcision party as they fell prey to their false teaching. Seducing spirits often accompany false teachings, leading them away from obeying the truth.

Our teachings (doctrines) often become the gospel we preach. An acquaintance of mine once said of himself, "I preach faith." Then he declared, "It works." However, the apostle Paul proclaimed that he preached Christ and Him crucified. Jesus is what *works* and Jesus is not an *it*. How astonishing that faith, the appropriate solution to the law, could be so skillfully turned back into law. Many well-meaning and God-seeking believers have been mesmerized by that false teaching.

Some denominations have made water baptism and membership into their *church* the way of salvation. Consequently, people are being inadvertently baptized into the name of that *church* rather than into the name of Jesus. What an affront to Jesus who plainly said, "I am the way, the truth, and the life. No man comes unto the Father but by Me." John 14:6.

Any practice, teaching, doctrine, ritual, program, rule, regulation, system, organization, association, or *church* government that binds and oppresses people rather than setting them free in Christ is not of God. It is legalism. Legalism is fleshly. Flesh is manipulative. Manipulation is the practice of witchcraft—manipulating others to do things against their will. We can be certain that wherever witchcraft is practiced, the demons of witchcraft colonize.

Chapter 16

The Demons of Witchcraft

$\mathcal{M}$ilton Green rightly observed that, in every situation there is either a Holy Spirit atmosphere or a demon atmosphere.

Whenever we have one of these Things we call *church*, it is a work of flesh. If flesh, then it is idolatrous. If idolatrous, then it is demon infested. If demon infested, then it is going to be driven by manipulation and control which is the practice of witchcraft in the broad and more subtle definition of the term. If it is the practice of witchcraft, then the demons of witchcraft will be swarming. Though they come in various degrees of strengths—every one of these Things will most likely have some demonic power or principality assigned to rule over it. The stench of flesh attracts the demons of witchcraft.

THE SPIRIT OF BABYLON

Spiritual Babylon takes on tangible form in this Thing we call *church. Church* is idolatrous. In the Bible, demons are associated with idolatry. The Lord spoke to Moses in Leviticus 17:7 regarding the Israelites saying, "They shall no more offer their sacrifices unto devils, after whom they have gone a whoring." So, too, this Thing we call *church* is possessed with demons—all the demons of spiritual Babylon.

I believe that the foremost of the demons of spiritual Babylon is the spirit of Babylon itself. (During the time of the Persian rule over Babylon, Daniel identified the prince of the Kingdom of Persia. Daniel 10:13. This "prince" is understood by the scriptural context to be a demonic stronghold over Persia.) I cannot say if there is one spirit of Babylon overall or if there are multitudes. I can say it is a very real presence in the *churches*.

The spirit of Babylon works in concert with the spirit of witchcraft and is monstrous in nature and in size. I was born and raised in spiritual Babylon as were many in the *church*. It was all I knew. It was in me, and I was in it. As a minister in that system, I found identity, significance, validation, power, support, and hope. It was a major stronghold in my life.

Even after my conversion and separation from the system, I

experienced times when I would be overcome by this spirit of Babylon. I wanted to go back into the system—the very thing that had spiritually bankrupted me before. The pull was so compelling at times that I was certain it was the voice of God calling me. The call contradicted the revelations and understandings I had been given about the *church* system, but I could not see the truth while under its veil of deception. After a while, that veil would lift and I would come to my senses.

Afterwards, I would feel guilty for having succumbed to that spirit. I thought to myself, "I must be awful." The Holy Spirit graciously gave me understanding. He showed me that this spirit of Babylon that came upon me was huge, and I was being overcome by it. It took years for me to be delivered from it. Even then, hoping to find me in a moment of weakness, its diminishing, seductive voice would call, "Come home."

THE UNHOLY TRINITY

When this Babylonian spirit is further exposed, I believe three other main demonic influences are seen working in concert with each other to take rule over carnal *churches*. They are a matriarchal spirit, a Jezebel spirit, and a spirit of witchcraft. These spirits operate as three in one to form the "unholy trinity" in opposition to the Father, Son, and Holy Spirit.

Matriarchal spirit. The matriarchal spirit is a counterfeit to Father-God. According to Merriam-Webster's Collegiate Dictionary/ Thesaurus, a matriarch is "a female who rules or dominates a family...the mother who is the head and ruler of her family and descendants." Revelation 17:5-6 reveals that this "MYSTERY, BABYLON THE GREAT," is called, "THE MOTHER OF HARLOTS..." This mother in Revelation is a matriarchal spirit. She is without a husband, has offspring, and rules over those offspring. Her offspring are called harlots. She has many of them.

The matriarchal spirit is most noted by this: she takes over. She dominates her house. She takes over the rule of everyone in her grasp. She takes over decision-making. She takes over conversations. She answers for other people. She takes over other people's lives. Those under her thumb are diminished, suffocated, and lose their identity into her. She mothers; she smothers. This domination occurs everywhere—in society, in the home, and particularly in the *church*. It is grossly out of divine order wherever it happens, but is especially grievous to God when it takes place among the household of God who build for themselves these Things we call *church*.

The matriarchal spirit usurps the role of the patriarch so she can make the household her own. She gains control over her house by means of the Jezebel spirit.

Jezebel. The Jezebel (harlot) spirit is a counterfeit to the Son, Jesus. The Jezebel spirit uses any means possible to entangle us in her web of bondage. She spins her witchcraft to accomplish this.

Witchcraft. The spirit of witchcraft is a counterfeit to the Holy Spirit. Witchcraft is, among many other things, seductive, enticing, deceptive, pushy, fear-arousing, shaming, manipulative, controlling, guilt-provoking, and hurtful.

Given time, this unholy trinity will take dominion in every harlot *church* system situation.

EMPOWERING THE MATRIARCHAL SPIRIT

These three manifestations work together as one. They have different functions, but work to achieve the same ultimate goal—to give dominion of the household over to the matriarchal spirit.

They counterfeit the functions of the Father, Son, and Holy Spirit. Just as the Holy Spirit's function is to glorify the Son, witchcraft's function is to help Jezebel achieve her goals. Just as Jesus came to glorify the Father, Jezebel's function is to ultimately empower/glorify the matriarchal spirit. Jezebel practices gendercide upon men (the masculine) in order to eliminate the patriarchs, leaving the rule of the house in the grip of the matriarchal spirit alone.

These three—the matriarch, Jezebel, and witchcraft—are so enmeshed that when the Jezebel spirit comes of age, so to speak, it turns into the matriarch. This happened to Bob and Sharon. Bob was called to serve the body of Christ full-time, but from the first day of their marriage onward, this matriarchal-Jezebel-witchcraft spirit, working through Sharon, opposed him on nearly every decision he tried to make. This spirit tried to dictate his life and ministry for him. It could not allow him to take the lead in their marriage though he was quite capable of doing so. As the years passed, it wore him down spiritually, emotionally, mentally, and physically. It became easier for him to give into it just to keep the peace than to repeatedly stand against it. Its need to dominate was the Jezebel in her. The way it came against him was the witchcraft in her. By the time they reached their sixties, witchcraft had worn him down, Jezebel had cut him off, and the matriarchal had taken him over. The Jezebel spirit within her transformed into the matriarch.

What happened to Bob and Sharon portrays what often takes place in the *church* system. For example: The pastor who *wants* domination over "his" sheep *suppresses* their gifts and ministries that he might have the *rule* over them. He *wants*—that's Jezebel; he *suppresses*—that witchcraft; he *rules*—that's the matriarch. This unholy trinity is gender-non-specific. It operates through male or female to secure its domination over its house. The true Patriarch over the ekklesia of God is Father-God. Anytime His people submit to any other spiritual authority for headship, the matriarch takes over whether the leadership is male or female.

The *church* system as a whole is structured for this unrighteous domination of a few people over many people. Phil Perry says regarding the harlot *church* system that "it will either make you domineering or keep you weak." Witchcraft and Jezebel in these Things we call *church* scheme to empower some people with ungodly authority and imprison others under that ungodly authority.

THE WOMAN IN THE BASKET

The passage in Zechariah 5:5-11 concerning the "woman in the basket" is a picture of this unholy trinity.

An angel showed Zechariah a basket (ephah which is a dry measure vessel), and Zechariah observed that the appearance of the basket went forth throughout the whole earth.

The basket is like the *church* system which indeed has gone forth throughout the whole earth.

The angel lifted a lid of lead off of the basket, allowing Zechariah to see a woman in it. The angel identified the woman as "Wickedness."

This Wickedness is like the matriarchal spirit that seeks to rule the *churches*. She is the personification of wickedness, the carnal mind, the abomination that makes the holy place (us) desolate, standing where it ought not. Mark 13:14.

The angel cast a lid of lead upon the mouth of the basket to hide her away. (Lead is heavy and is like the heaviness that is felt whenever the matriarchal spirit is present.) The angel thereby shut her up for a period of time.

The matriarchal spirit in the *churches* has been hidden until now, but will soon be revealed when she seats herself upon the throne in her own house.

Then Zechariah saw two women coming with the wind in their wings. Their wings were like those of a stork.

The two women are like the Jezebel and witchcraft spirits that work in concert with the matriarchal spirit.

These two women lifted up the basket with the woman, Wickedness, in it and took it to Shinar which is Babylon.

Shinar is like the Babylonian captivity of the *church*; namely, the harlot *church* system.

The two women took the basket to Shinar to build a house for Wickedness. It will be her own house, and it will be established. Once it is established, she will be put on her own pedestal (base, resting place, foundation). She will be the head of it.

The Jezebel and witchcraft spirits took this woman to Shinar, the place of the harlot *church* system, to build a house for her. Her house is a counterfeit to the temple of the Holy Spirit—all true believers—over which Christ is the head. When this house was prepared, Wickedness, the matriarchal spirit, would be set on her pedestal, apparently to receive all things to herself that she might be all in all. This counterfeits the destiny of Jesus who, when all things have been subjected to Him, shall also be subjected to God that God may be all in all. 1 Cor. 15:28.

This plot by the unholy trinity is being carried out to fulfillment in the harlot *church* system today: the Jezebel spirit is being transformed into the matriarch.

DRONES OF WITCHCRAFT

These three main demonic strongholds sit like queen bees with a swarm of drones to do their bidding. The angel in Revelation 18:2 "cried mightily with a strong voice, saying, 'Babylon the great is fallen, is fallen, and is become the habitation of *devils*, and the hold of every *foul spirit*, and a cage of every *unclean and hateful bird.*'" The foul spirit and the unclean and hateful bird speak of demons.

Paul wrote, "Now the Spirit speaks expressly, that in the latter times some shall depart from the faith, giving heed to seducing spirits, and the doctrines of devils." 1 Tim. 4:1. He later added that "the time will come when they will not endure sound doctrine, but after their own lusts shall they heap to themselves teachers, having itching ears. And they shall turn away their ears from the truth, and shall be turned to fables." 2 Tim. 4:3-4. Demons whisper into our itching ears, and we succumb to their deceits when we have not settled the issue of utter surrender to the lordship of Jesus Christ. We still lust for Self and do not love the truth.

Remember, the Lord was talking to the assemblies of the called-out-ones in Asia when He mentioned the doctrine of Balaam in Revelation 2:14, the doctrine of the Nicolaitans in Revelation 2:15, and the doctrine of Jezebel in Revelation 2:24. These were false teachings that threatened the simplicity and purity of the devotion of the saints to Jesus.

These *church* demons are very real and work in concert with each other to create havoc within the body of Christ. These unseen puppeteers manipulate our strings to create deception, confusion, division, bigotry, and hatred.

Church demons lie and deceive us to the point that we can become bound to these Things we call *church.* Even though we know we are in bondage to these spiritually dead Things, we and demons can come up with the most elaborate justifications for staying in them. "But who will preach my funeral?" "My children have friends here." "I was born, baptized, and married in here." "Granddaddy helped to build this church."

THE NAMES OF DEMONS

"Abolish Sunday School!" And so I did. The decision to do so was not easy, nor was it without consequences. It cost me my job in the small, rural *church* where I had just begun to preach. I had no idea in the beginning that demons would be unearthed in such a decision, but I soon found out. The Lord exposed a golden calf in the hearts of some of the people. Through these three simple words, "abolish Sunday School," the Lord exposed a few people who were joined to a tradition of men, who by their own confessions and choices showed that they loved the institution of Sunday School too much to "test the Spirit" in the matter.

In this process, God exposed numerous deeds of the flesh among the core dissenters. Each deed of the flesh italicized below had a corresponding demonic spirit that went with it. Demons are named according to their activities.

Their doctrines and governmental policies were *restrictive,* disallowing the Holy Spirit to do a new thing among them. Any thought or action that did not fit into the narrow corridor of their *church* polity was rejected. Anyone who dared to test those boundaries was thought to be an adversary to the faith. Thus, demons of restriction were present.

They were *possessive* in their attempt to own the property, the pulpit, the program, and the people. Thus, demons of possessiveness were present.

Their possessiveness made them *manipulative* and *controlling* which was the practice of *witchcraft.* Demons of manipulation, control, and witchcraft were present.

Two of the elders were deceptive when they went in stealth without my knowledge to the higher authorities in an attempt to oust me. Demons of deception were present.

They were *rebellious* against hearing a word of the Lord. They did not pretend to be speaking for the Lord, but were standing on their tradition. Consequently, they were *stubborn, stiff-necked,* and *unyielding.* Change was not an option. Their stubbornness was *prideful* and *arrogant.* Stiff-necked demons and demons of rebellion, pride, and arrogance were present.

They were *idolatrous* in that they loved their *church* and tradition more than their willingness to trust and obey the Holy Spirit. Their identities were wrapped up in their *church.* Demons of idolatry were present.

They were *legalistic, political, clannish, unforgiving, suspicious, jealous, impudent, slanderous, petty, spiteful,* and *contentious.* All of those demons were present as well.

If we are sectarian, there will be spirits of *sectarianism;* if we are divisive, there will be spirits of *division;* if we are legalistic, there will be spirits of *legalism;* if we are religious, there will be spirits of *religion;* if we are seductive, there will spirits of *seduction;* if we are jealous, there will be spirits of *jealousy;* if we are unforgiving, there will be spirits of *unforgiveness;* if we are hateful, there will be spirits of *hate;* if we lust, there will be spirits of *lust;* if we are power hungry, there will be spirits of *intimidation* and *domination;* if we have malice and murder in our hearts, there will be spirits of *malice* and *murder.*

Murder!? A murderous spirit in the *church!?* It can be in the heart. Pastor Henry had lost favor with many of his parishioners. They called for a vote to fire him and he won by a narrow margin. To the surprise of his congregation the following Sunday, he confessed from the pulpit that he would have killed everyone who voted against him had he a gun. The Catholic Inquisition in the 1500s is one among many historical examples of how horrifying this spirit of murder can be in the name of "Christianity." Church officials held secret trials and turned condemned heretics over to secular governments to be burned. Jesus was tried, convicted, and executed by the murderous religious leaders of His day. (They killed Him only because He willingly laid down His life.) If we are seeking something for Self, we will despise those who threaten us. Some would kill if they could.

The demons in the *churches* are many and vicious. Many *churches* have become more of the battlefield for injury than a triage center for healing.

DEMONS AND PEOPLE

Demons can only work through willing people. Evil spirits have legal access to those who commit sin. The practice of control and manipulation is sin and opens the door to spirits of witchcraft.

Those who rule within these Things we call *church* may be few in number, perhaps only one. It may be the pastor, but not necessarily. In most denominations, pastors move around from *church* to *church*, limiting their ability to get much of a stronghold over their congregations. Those pastors who gain such a stronghold in their *church* are generally those who stay there a lifetime or those who actually chartered a *church* in their own name.

Quite often, those in control are "lay" persons who not only rule the *church*, but control the pastors as well. They may be male or female. The matriarchal influence may be in Miss Neesie whose ancestors founded the *church*, and nothing is ever done there without her approval. The Jezebel influence may be in Jennifer who seduced Pastor John into having an affair with her, or it may be in Pastor John who seduced Jennifer into having an affair with him. The witchcraft influence may be in deacon Will who controls the purse strings, or it may be in self-appointed prophetess Charlotte who manipulates people's lives through false prophecies. Many times rulers in the *churches* are those who have money and position in the community and thereby intimidate others who unduly revere them.

One pastor friend of mine told me years ago that when he went to a new *church* situation, his first task was to discover who the "chief" was in order to find a way to work with him or her.

WITCHCRAFT AND THE HOLY SPIRIT

One way to discern this counterfeit spirit of witchcraft is to see it in contrast to the nature and work of the Holy Spirit.

Witchcraft is characterized by deceit; the Holy Spirit is characterized by honesty, truthfulness, and straightforwardness. God is Truth.

Witchcraft is ambitious; therefore, it is impatient and pushy. It has its own agenda and is not content to wait upon the Lord. The whole idea of waiting is threatening to the practice of witchcraft. If we cannot wait on God to bring a thing about, we are wanting something God has not ordained. If God ordained it, we should be able to wait for Him to bring it about in His timing. His timing is perfect. The nature of the Holy Spirit in us is to rest, wait, listen, and then act only when it is time to act. The Holy Sprit is patient, gentle, kind, and long-suffering.

Witchcraft deals in fear, anxiety, and restlessness. The Holy Spirit offers trust, faith, confidence, and rest in God.

Witchcraft creates an atmosphere that is negative and destructive. The Holy Spirit creates an atmosphere that is positive and uplifting.

Witchcraft bears the fruit of strife, poverty, and death. The Holy Spirit bears the fruit of peace, blessing, and life.

Witchcraft is characterized by one's attempt to control people and circumstances by speaking curses. The Holy Spirit calls forth that which is good by speaking blessings. With the tongue we can bless God or curse men. James 3:9.

Witchcraft is intrusive. The Holy Spirit is gentle.

Witchcraft is wicked. The Holy Spirit is righteous.

THE ROYAL LAW OF LIBERTY

James 1:25 refers to the perfect law of liberty. We have to let people be free. We have to let them be free to be who they are and where they are at any given point and time in their lives.

Any act of control that creates bondage for another person is the subtle practice of witchcraft. Jesus Christ is Truth. He is the way, the truth, and the life. John 14:6. "You shall know the truth and the truth shall make you free." John 8:32. "Where the Spirit of the Lord is, there is liberty." 2 Cor. 3:17. "It was for freedom, Christ set us free." Gal. 5:1.

The flesh nature of man is naturally prone to manipulation and control which is the practice of witchcraft. Therefore, it is under the influence of the demons of witchcraft. When witchcraft is present, the Jezebel demon is present. When the Jezebel demon is present, the Ahab (Nicolaitan) demon is present. When these demons are in operation within the carnal *church*, we have what Jesus called in Revelation "the deep things of Satan."

Chapter 17

The Deep Things of Satan

"*How* are you fallen from heaven, O Lucifer, son of the morning? How are you cut down to the ground...For you have said in your heart, 'I will ascend into heaven, I will exalt my throne above the stars of God, I will sit also upon the mount of the congregation, in the sides of the north. I will ascend above the heights of the clouds. I will be like the most High." Isa. 14:12-13.

THE DWELLING PLACE OF SATAN

Several things of interest are revealed to us in the above verses of scripture from Isaiah. First, we note that this reference to Lucifer, whom I believe is Satan, is in the context of the prophecy of the fall of the king of Babylon and of the destruction of Babylon. Isa. 14:3-11,22-23. If we remove the subheadings and the chapters and verses that have arbitrarily been given to these verses, they read as one continuous passage, thus linking Lucifer with Babylon as the king of Babylon.

Secondly, we note that Lucifer made five boasts, five "I wills." He seeks to usurp the place of God in heaven, to exalt his throne above the stars, to sit upon the mount of the congregation in the sides of the north, to ascend above the heights of the clouds, and to be like the most High. This is what Babylon is about—the exaltation of Self. It is all that the carnal mind devises.

Thirdly and most particularly, Lucifer said he would sit also upon the mount of the congregation in the sides of the north. Psalms 48:2 lets us know that "the sides of the north" refers to Mount Zion: "Beautiful for situation, the joy of the whole earth, is Mount Zion, on the sides of the north, the city of the great King." The "great King" in this verse refers to Yahweh who is Jesus. Psalms 2:6 declares, "Yet have I set My king upon My holy hill of Zion." Zion is God's dwelling place (Ps. 9:11) and is "the city of the great king." Zion is also a type of God's holy remnant. "Remember Your congregation who You have purchased of old, the rod of Your inheritance who You have redeemed, this Mount Zion, wherein You dwell." Ps. 74:2. Also we read, "They who trust in the Lord shall be as Mount Zion." Ps. 125.1. Lucifer intended from the beginning of time to seat himself as the head of the congregation of God's people.

Israel was the congregation of God's people, as are all true believers in Christ to this day. Lucifer sought to be the head of Israel then, just as he seeks to be the head of the body of Christ to this day. Luke 4:13 reads, "And when the devil had ended all the temptation, he departed from Him [Jesus] for a season." But only for a season—Satan wasted no time to deceive, if possible, the elect of God. Matt. 24:24. His takeover of the *churches* should be no surprise to us.

We read in the book of Revelation how involved Satan was in three of the assemblies of called-out-ones that are mentioned there. He, not Jesus, was ruling their hearts. Jesus was standing and knocking outside of the door, spiritually speaking, of the ekklesia in Laodicea saying, "...if any man hear My voice and opens the door, I will come into to him and will sup with him, and he with Me." Rev. 2:20.

SATAN'S SEAT

The Lord Jesus instructed the apostle John to write to the called-out-ones in Pergamos saying, "He who has the sharp sword with two-edges, I know your works and where you dwell, *where Satan's seat is.*" Rev. 2:13. The interpretation of this phrase, *where Satan's seat is*, is not clear. Is Satan's seat [throne] in the middle of this assembly of called-out-ones? Does he have his throne in the same city where they are? Or, are there simply people in the assembly at Pergamos who represent Satan's actions? It says that his seat is there and then says that he dwells there. This agrees with Satan's own aspiration to seat himself also upon "the mount of the congregation, in the sides of the north." Whichever is the case, he stirred up persecution among them. Jesus commended those who upheld His name and did not deny the faith. Nevertheless, He held a few things against them because they had some *among* them who followed the teachings of Balaam and the Nicolaitans.

Satan was in the middle of all of this. It would be naive to think that Satan could be elsewhere. His mission has always been to wage war against Jesus Christ, the Son of the living God, and His assembly of called-out-ones. Whatever else he does in the world, he does it in order to try to embarrass, usurp, or dethrone Jesus or to rob Him of His inheritance in the saints. Eph. 1:18. Satan will not set up his throne outside of the encampments of God's people unless he must. Unfortunately, because of people's fleshly ways and harlot hearts, he has been given free room and board to camp within. He positions himself as close to the center of God's people as he can.

THE DEEP THINGS OF SATAN

Jesus began His message through John to the called-out-ones in Thyatira by recognizing their works, love, service, faith, patience, and that their last works were more than the first. Then He said He was against them for tolerating that woman Jezebel who called herself a prophetess. She taught and seduced His servants to commit fornication and to eat things sacrificed to idols. Jesus had even given her time to repent, but she did not. Consequently, He said He would cast her into a sickbed and would cast those who committed adultery with her into great tribulation; that is, unless they repented of their deeds. Moreover, Jesus said He would kill Jezebel's children with death so that all of the called-out-ones would know that He is the one who searches the inner hearts of men and gives to everyone according to their works. Jezebel's spiritual children are those who follow her in deception and idolatry. Jesus made a distinction here between Jezebel's children and His own called-out-ones. Then Jesus said He would put no other burden upon the rest of them in Thyatira, "as many as have not this doctrine [teaching] and who have not known *the deep things of Satan*." Rev. 2:18-29.

That there were those in the assembly of called-out-ones in Thyatira who did not know the deep things of Satan suggests that there were those in the assembly who did know. These were those who allowed themselves to be seduced by Jezebel to commit fornication and to eat things sacrificed to idols.

Jesus charged those who had not known these deep things of Satan to hold fast to what they had until He came. Why would He have told them to hold fast to what they had? Because that which they had could be easily taken from them by deception. This Jezebel spirit is very seductive and deceiving.

Jezebel was in the assembly of called-out-ones in Thyatira and had followers. She was teaching things that Jesus called "the deep things of Satan." Nothing could be clearer. If these Things we call *church* are idolatrous extensions of self-worship—flesh—then those who rule over them practice witchcraft and are under the control of the spirits of witchcraft; and if under witchcraft, then they too are involved in the deep things of Satan.

SYNAGOGUES OF SATAN

When Jesus charged John to write the assemblies in Smyrna and Philadelphia, He mentioned those who blasphemed by calling themselves Jews, whom Jesus clarified were not Jews but were the synagogue of Satan. Rev. 2:8-9; 3:7-9. Jesus could have been referring to some Judaizers who might have penetrated the ranks of the believers there, but it is more likely that He was referring to unconverted Jews who slandered the believers in these cities.

Jesus said those who falsely called themselves Jews were the synagogue of Satan. Just as believers are the temple of the Holy Spirit, they were the synagogue [gathering place] of Satan—not their buildings, beliefs, or activities. He said that they blasphemed by calling themselves Jews.

Paul taught that the true Jews are followers of Jesus. "For he is not a Jew who is one outwardly, neither is that circumcision which is outward in the flesh. But he is a Jew who is one inwardly, and circumcision is that of the heart, in the spirit, and not in the letter, whose praise is not of men, but of God." Rom. 2:28-29.

They were synagogues of Satan because they opposed and persecuted the followers Jesus. They had already determined in the synagogues that any man who confessed that Jesus was of Christ should be put out of the synagogue. John 9:22. So much stress was put on belonging to the synagogue that it was shameful to be put out of it. Guilt and shame were applied as a means of manipulating, controlling, dominating, and possessing the constituents of the synagogue, just as it is done in *churches* today. It is a hard saying, but whoever allows the flesh to rule rather than the Holy Spirit, they, too, are the synagogue of Satan.

THE TRUE PATTERN

Most everyone agrees that the *church* system from its inception after the first century A.D. has been patterned after the synagogue system of the Jewish religion. The word synagogue literally means a bringing together. It was the place the Jews gathered to read and explain the sacred scriptures and pray, but it became more than a gathering place. It became both a building and an institution just as it is with *church* today. Some similarities between the synagogue and *church* systems are footnoted below with personal comments.[23]

---

[23]Factual sources below were abstracted from *Harper's Bible Dictionary* and *Nelson's New Illustrated Bible Dictionary*, s.v. "synagogue."

Origin. The origin of the synagogue as an institution is not certain. Though synagogues are not specifically mentioned in the Old Testament, they came into existence sometime after Judah was taken into Babylonian captivity in the 6th century B.C. Babylon was a likely place for them to have begun.

By New Testament times, synagogues had become numerous and were playing a larger role in community life. They were social centers for Jewish activities and schools for their children. They might have been used as local courts and for scourging. At least Jesus predicted that they would do such things in their synagogues against those that He would send. Matt 10:17; 23:34.

As far as scriptural evidence goes, there is no mention of God instituting synagogues, just as Jesus did not institute *church* as we know of it today. Both the synagogue and *church*, for whatever good intentions they may serve, are still the institutions of men and the outgrowth of men's traditions.

Buildings. The Jews may have first "synagogued" in homes, but evidence shows that they erected buildings for themselves early on. The remains of one has been identified in Alexandria, Egypt, which is thought to date back to around 230 B.C. Jewish synagogues were well established throughout the Roman Empire and were in Jerusalem by the time of Jesus. The earliest type of architecture was the basilica. The basilica has a central nave (the main part) with a semicircular apse (a projection of the building), two or four side aisles, a narthex (vestibule or entry area), and a clerestory (high walls with windows over the nave). The Torah was placed in an ark (cabinet) on a platform where there were also lamps and a lectern.

Many *churches* are still patterned after the basilica style of architecture. The only buildings God commissioned were the Tabernacle of Moses which was a movable tent with articles in it and Solomon's temple. Exod. 25:8-9 and 1 Chron. 28. Christians did not build their own places of worship until Emperor Constantine was converted around 325 A.D. and Christianized the entire Roman empire.

Seating. The younger people sat in the back while the best seats up front were reserved for the elders. Jesus condemned this prideful lust for prominence in Matthew 23:6. Referring to the scribes and Pharisees, He said that they loved the chief seats in the synagogues. Clergy still love the chief seats in their congregations. Those platform chairs are typically large, elaborate, and upholstered for royalty.

Officials. A synagogue could not be formed unless there were at least ten Jewish men in the community. Jesus said that where two or more are gathered in His name, there He would be in the midst of them. Matt. 18:20. The synagogues had a board of devoted and respected *elders* who regulated the policies of the synagogue. One or more men were elected by the elders to be the *ruler(s)* of the synagogue. The rulers took care of the building and planned the services. A *minister* was in charge of the sacred scrolls, attended the lamps, kept the building clean, did the prescribed scourging, and taught the children during the week. The ruler appointed a *delegate of the congregation* to read the Scripture lesson, to lead in prayer, and to preach or comment on the scripture. The Torah was written in ancient Hebrew so an *interpreter* was often needed. Two or three *almoners* (one who distributes charity) took up money or other necessities for the poor.

The fact that Jesus habitually went to the synagogue, read from the scroll, and taught is not an endorsement of the synagogue system. Luke 4:16-20 records that Jesus was even driven out of the synagogue. In Matthew 10:17 and 13:54, Jesus and Matthew referred to them as *their* synagogues.

Different traditions of Christian *churches* have variations of these officers. In the Presbyterian system, the board of elders rule along with the pastors. They are equivalent to the *minister* in the synagogue. Deacons or ushers are selected to receive and count the offerings. They are the equivalent to the *almoners*. The ruling officers may be called deacons as in the Baptist tradition or may be priests as in the Episcopal tradition.

Paul recognized that God gave some to be apostles, some prophets, some evangelists, some shepherds (who are the elder-overseers), and some teachers. The King James Version used the term "office" when it generally should have been translated service. Rom. 11:13; 12:4; 1 Tim. 3:1; 3:10; and 3:13. The idea of ministry being an office or position is foreign to New Testament thought. It is not a New Testament term or distinction. These are functions—acts of servanthood—in the body of Christ. No such "positions" exist in the Kingdom of God, only in the kingdoms of men.

Order of worship. Before the service, the minister would place the Torah on the lectern and scroll it to the reading for the day. The service began with the *Shema*—the passage in Deuteronomy 6:4-9. The speaker for the day led in prayer—facing Jerusalem with hands extended—after which the people said, "Amen." He stood up to read the lesson for the day and sat down to sermonize upon it. Luke 4:20. Afterwards, if a priest were present, he would pronounce the benediction to which the people said, "Amen." If no priest were present, someone offered a closing prayer. The scriptures are still read and sermons are still preached in the *churches* today much as they were in the synagogues, following prescribed lectionaries for the week.

This format is in stark contradiction to the spirit-led, believer's meeting which the New Testament followers had, going from house to house. The Corinthians' meeting are pictured in 1 Corinthians 14:26: "How is it then, brothers? When you come together, everyone of you has a psalm, has a doctrine, has a tongue, has a revelation, has an

The Pharisees were an inseparable part of the synagogue system by the time of Jesus and were distinguished by their legalism; their lust for power, position, recognition, and dominance; their stiff-necked attitudes; their self-righteousness and hypocrisy; their self-seeking lifestyle; and their murderous intentions.

What are we to say of those clergy persons in present-day Christendom who are likewise legalistic; who lust for power, position, recognition, and dominance; who are stiff-necked, self-righteous, hypocritical, and self-seeking; and who have murderous intentions in their hearts? Might they be modern-day Pharisees in the *churches!?*

Make this connection with me. If the leaders of that Thing you are in that you call *church* have the marks of the Pharisees, they are in the flesh and seeking something for themselves. They are the synagogue of Satan. If you participate in, share in, and have your fellowship with them in that idolatrous system, it is most likely because the system is in your heart as well. If that is the case, you are the synagogue of Satan with them. Satan has his synagogue and Jesus has His assembly of called-out-ones. We are the called-out-ones for assembly into Him. He formed a people. He is building His temple and it is made up of lively stones. We are to be joined only to Him. Bill Shipman observes, "If we are joined, submitted, committed, or covenanted to anyone or anything other than to the Lord Jesus Christ, we are committing spiritual adultery."

Much of what Jesus taught was in contradiction to what the Pharisees stood for. He figuratively pointed a finger at the Pharisees, declaring to His disciples, "See them? What they say and do is not it. Look at Me! I am the way and the truth and the life..." We have patterned that which we call *church* after the synagogue system of men. The true assembly of called-out-ones can never be patterned after a Thing. The bride of Christ can never be defined by systems, institutions, buildings, governmental orders, programs, formulas, creeds, doctrines, rituals, and litanies. The assembly of called-out-ones is a people who are patterned after the person,

---

interpretation..." New Testament assemblies were characterized by the existence of the equipping gift ministries of apostles, prophets, evangelists, pastors (elders) and teachers; by the plurality of elders; by the operation of all of the gifts of the Holy Spirit; and by mutual recognition of one another's contribution to the body of Christ. Jesus said the Father was seeking those who would worship Him in Spirit and in truth (John 4:23-24), not according to a bulletin or dead ritual.

I am convinced beyond doubt that if Jesus were to walk into most of the *churches* today, He would be treated much the same as He was in the synagogues in His day. The difference between what He called us to and what we have in *church* today is striking.

Jesus Christ. He alone is the governor and the government of the Kingdom of God. Isa. 9:6.

When it comes to this Thing we call *church*, in most cases, Satan has positioned himself and his throne in the middle of it. We must see that! His deception is so great that we do not even know we may be serving him amidst our service to Christ. "For Satan himself is transformed into an angel of light." 2 Cor. 11:14. He is false light who is full of deception and deep darkness. This Thing we call *church* veils the eyes of those who remain a party to *it*. People are so deceived by this darkness that they have innocently become the dispensers of it. *Church*, in all of its darkness, is the counterfeit harlot to the true bride.

The harlot *church* system springs forth from those who have spiritual Babylon in their hearts. This Babylon is the great whore that sits on many waters. "Many waters" includes all peoples of all nations in all denominations and non-denominational *churches* who practice the harlotry of *church*.

OUTSIDE THE CAMP

The harlot *church* system cannot be fixed. It can never be redeemed. It is flesh and all flesh is under the domain of Satan. God's people—we who are called by His name and who do not allow ourselves to be called by any other name—must come out of Babylon. We are redeemed by the blood of the Lamb, joined to Him only, baptized into His death, and raised in His resurrection. We are immersed in and led by His Holy Sprit. He alone is the Lord of our lives. We are submitted one to another in the spirit of humility and love.

Bob Hughey writes, "God is looking for a people, not a place. His building program is made up of living stones, not concrete blocks, lumber, and nails. He is looking for and raising up a people of faith, not some theological meeting to come up with a statement of faith. He is not starting a new non-profit organization, He is bringing to life a living organism with true apostles, prophets, evangelists, pastors and teachers, and with everyone in the body a minister. He is not looking for a people known by their doctrine, pastor's name, location, but is raising up a people known by their love for Him and for one another. He is not looking for a people bound by traditions, but is raising up a people free in Jesus and being led by His Holy Spirit."[24]

---

[24]James Nesbit, *A Lifestyle of Light*, 2nd ed. (Liberty, TN: Hughey and Nesbit,1999), 350.

"Wherefore Jesus also, that He might sanctify the people with His own blood, suffered outside the gate. Let us go forth therefore unto Him outside the camp, bearing His reproach." Heb. 13:12-13.

Chapter 18

Who Shall Ascend?[25]

I called upon the name of the Lord, "Who, Lord, shall ascend to the high mountain of our God and King?"

He answered, "He who has a broken and contrite heart. He who humbles himself in My presence. He is the one who shall ascend unto My holy hill." And I called again and I asked, "Lord, how does one humble himself? Man is so full of pride."

And He said, "He who humbles himself is he who recognizes his pride and breaks before Me. I will see him. I will come to him. I will break his heart. He will weep and mourn for he will know that he is a man of unclean lips. I will see him and I will lift him up. But if he lifts himself up, I will let him fall again."

I asked again, "Lord, where do we go from here?"

And He answered, "Where do you want to go? Whatever is in your heart, that is where you will go. If it is in your heart to follow after Me, then we will walk together and abide in deeper and richer things. We will go from glory to glory, from faith to faith. Yes, we will ascend and ascend, every round going higher and higher. This, My son, is a place in Me. I am Mount Zion. I am My holy hill. When I say come unto Me, I am calling you up to My high hill.

"If, on the other hand, it is in your heart to go down to Babylon or back to Egypt, then you shall go there. The rewards of Babylon will be there and the jewels of Egypt will be yours. Only do not trust in them for they cannot save you, and in that hour when I come in all My glory, do not try to ransom your soul with them. They are vile to Me. I shall cast them away from you. I shall strip you naked and leave you in your shame.

"There is glory in Babylon and there are riches in Egypt, but they will go down to the pit. For from the pit have they ascended. They are flesh and appeal to the flesh. Do not touch them. Do not go after them, for surely they shall be yours if you like."

---

[25] I have included this prophecy which I received on February 4, 1987, because it serves as a thorough summary of and closure to the preceding chapters.

"Lord," I inquired, "this is a great deception isn't it—Babylon and Egypt?"

"There has never been a greater deception than this," He answered.

I shuddered at the thought of this.

"So great is this deception," He explained, "that men go down to Babylon, adorn themselves in religion and piety, and truly believe that they have come unto Me. They are shaken to anger at the suggestion that this, their Babylon, is not of Me, that I am not there.

"And Egypt, what can I say of My son, Egypt? He, too, is beautiful and rich and dwells in houses and owns land and buys and trades and sells in the marketplace. The prosperity abounds and so does the deception. For in their riches they live and move and have their being. But where will their riches get them, and what will it buy them when I come? I will look the poor man in the eye and see from whence came his hunger. I will look the rich man in the eye and ask from whence came his satisfaction, and he will be lifted up in his heart, and he will show Me all the things in his barns and say, 'My Lord, from all that is mine.' I will turn again to the poor man, and I will ask from whence came your poverty, and he will point to the rich man's barn and say, 'My Lord, from all that is his.' From whence comes your satisfaction? The poor man will bow and say, 'Ah, my Lord, from You; from You, my Lord, from You.'"

I said, "Lord, speak plainly to us. What is Babylon and what is Egypt?"

He answered, "Babylon is all that the carnal mind devises. It is the pride and arrogance and the haughtiness of man who exalts his own knowledge above the knowledge of God.

"As for Egypt, this is the flesh and all the lust thereof.

"Can you not see, My son, how the carnal mind has devised his own plan with all its traditions and labeled it *church*? For generations men thought this was of Me and for Me, but it is not so. This is the harlot, the woman who sits on many waters, who pretends allegiance to Me, but she is widowed. She is not My bride. Her deception is great. She has attained for herself the riches of this world. She has lavished herself with fine buildings and calls them temples and cathedrals and synagogues and churches. She has dressed herself in royal robes which she wove by her own hands. The linen I give is righteousness which has been purchased by My blood. She has accrued great riches with bank accounts and investments and have men bound to her by these things. She has purchased these things by the blood of martyrs.

"Everywhere you look, you can see the harlot. She is every-where in men's hearts. Men go after her, and she loves it so. She is not married, but has taken unto herself many lovers. She is defiled and those who sleep with her are defiled.

"Mercy and peace are with those who have eyes to see and ears to hear when the trumpets sound and the call goes forth, 'Come out of her, My people, come out!'

"The road to Zion is paved with humility."

"Lord," I cried, "it's so hard to say. Why is it so hard for me to say it plainly? Why is it so hard for you to say it plainly?"

He answered, "Because the deception is so great.

"Christianity is a religion, and religious men are caught in its web. Who can hear Me," said the Lord, "or who can hear My prophets when it is said of Christianity that it, as a religious system, is a false religion? Who can understand when I declare that all religion is false? The greatest deception of all is for men to come to it in My name, thinking they have come to Me. I am not an "it." I am not a religion. I am the living and true God. I require that men come unto Me and renounce all religion, but who can hear?

"Religion has boundaries. I am boundless. It has its laws and rules and regulations. I offer grace and love and peace. Religion binds men; I free them. Religion suppresses men; I call them to ascend into the heavenlies. Religion restrains and controls; I release. Religion requires obedience to it; I require obedience to Me. Yes, obedience is far better than sacrifices. I loathe religion and religious men. They are dangerous and spread the deception to innocent hearts."

"Lord, you have spoken plainly. So where shall they go who come out of Babylon?"

And He answered simply, "To Jesus."

"Ascend, My holy ones, ascend into the heavenlies. Sit at My right hand and at My left. I will show you mysteries. I will show you great and glorious things.

"You are My witnesses—My two witnesses—one on My left and the other on My right. On My left is grace and mercy and peace. And on My right is righteousness, justice, and wrath. I am a two-edged sword. My sword goes forth out of My mouth. It divides the righteous from the unrighteous. It is sharp and quick and sure.

"Behold, I am dividing right from wrong. I am making straight the path. I am exalting valleys. I am moving mountains. The high will be made low, and the low will be made high.

"If he cannot understand this (the man of sin), let him go down into his house, shut his door and weep and mourn, for surely pity shall come upon his house."

"How shall they come out of Babylon?" I asked the Lord.

"They shall come out by coming unto Me. Simply leave. The door is opened. The way is made clear. The prophets have gone before. Do not look back. Do not go back. Simply leave.

"And when they criticize you and call you blasphemous names, let your head be as flint; be silent; be at peace; love them; turn the other cheek, for they so persecuted your fathers before you.

"Do not look back. Do not do anything. Do not say anything. Simply leave. Say in your heart, 'I have left Babylon and have ascended the high hill of my God. I have come to Mount Zion, to Jesus, the author and finisher of My faith.'

"You cannot take Zion down to Babylon. You have to come out of her. You cannot sing Zion's songs in Babylon. They can only be sung in Zion.

"Zion is a place in the Spirit where Jesus is the only thing there is."

"Lord," my questions seemed endless, "this kind of freedom, this independence, this liberty—will it not be a great threat to those who lead in Babylon?"

"Oh yes, My son, they will take great offense at My holy ones. They will say you are deceived. They will slander, accuse, and defame you. They would plot to kill you if they could. For you, My holy ones, have become what they cannot, because they cannot let go of what they have. Yet, it shall all very soon be taken from them anyway."

"Tell me, Lord, in view of all of this, have we really heard the gospel yet? What is the gospel? Speak plainly to us."

"The gospel has been twisted and perverted to fit the molds of traditions and religions—so uniquely so, that men confuse the Christ with their systems and join converts to them rather than to Him.

"But the truth of the gospel is this: that I, the Lord God of Israel, came in human flesh, fulfilled the Law and Prophets, shed My blood of righteousness, arose from the grave, ascended into heaven where I now sit at the right hand of God the Father, where I intercede on behalf of the saints, and through faith am gathering unto

Myself My assembly of holy ones. They are gathered into Me. They are My general assembly of the first-born. I have birthed them by My Spirit. I have filled them with My Spirit. I lead them by My Spirit. They are one in faith, hope, spirit, and love. They are everywhere and worship Me in spirit and truth. In obedience they serve Me where they are, out of who they are in Me. And none of this has anything to do with that Thing men call *church*. They are My body, My temple, My holy ones, a royal priesthood, a holy nation. They are above institutionalism—beyond doctrines, creeds, and rituals. They are not religious. They are sanctified.

"This is the good news: that Jesus Christ is Lord. And whosoever shall call upon His name shall be saved."

"Lord, I know of young pastors, Spirit-filled, who love you and want to go on with you. What shall they do once they see these things?"

"No man having put his hands to the plow and looking back is fit for the kingdom of heaven."

"Again, I plead with you, my Lord, speak plainly."

And He said, "He who sees these things and obeys My word will simply come out. He will leave home and family and friends and come out. It is a hard word, who can hear?

"These are they who follow the Lamb wherever He goes." Rev. 14:4.

"Lord, what shall I do with this word?"

"Shout it from the housetops. Proclaim it to the nations. What has been revealed to you in secret, proclaim it in the open. Be bold! Be forthright! Be strong! Speak it boldly. Shock the nations. Rattle their doors. Shake their foundations. If they cannot stand, they are not of Me. If it can be shut down and closed up, it is not of Me. If it can be tossed by the wind, it is not of Me. If it produces anger and violence and malicious gossip and slanderings and lies from those who hear it, they are not of Me, for such things do not come out of Me.

"Behold, I have laid My foundation. I have built My walls. And now I am dropping My plumb line. My word of truth goes forth. That which does not align with My word will be torn down and cast into the sea. I am sending My prophets again. They go out in the spirit of Elijah, preaching the kingdom of God and calling men everywhere to repent and be immersed into Jesus. They are My "John the Baptists." They go forth to prepare the way of the Lord.

"Shall I return to wed a harlot? Oh, how repulsive that is to Me.

Nor shall I take unto Myself those who are joined to her. Search your hearts, My people. Babylon is in the heart. Come out of her and she will come out of you. Zion, likewise, is in the heart. Come unto Me and I will become your only love.

"Arise. Shine. Come unto Me."

"Lord," I prayed, "forgive me for the fear and the intimidation I feel when I think about speaking these things out."

"You shall know the harlot by this as well, that she has such a powerful control over the hearts and minds of men that they are laden with fear to dare come out of her, let alone speak against her. She is the epitome of idolatry and full of idolatry, and all those joined to her are idolaters. Now you must realize, My son, that a thing is an idol when men have put their trust and love in it. And idolaters do not want their idols touched. It is a dangerous thing to touch another man's idol. As you speak these things, you will be pulling down strongholds and shattering idols—and you will be hated by many for My name's sake.

"Now the harlot, the mother of harlots, is the spirit of Satan himself. He has hidden behind her skirt and deceived the nations. He is last of all willing for her to be exposed. He is, indeed, the great dragon and will try to consume My bond-servants, those I am sending forth in My name to proclaim the gospel of the kingdom and to expose the harlot and her counterfeits.

"A fierce war has begun in the heavenlies. All hell is loosed to destroy My bond-servants if they could, but they cannot even so much as touch them because they are dead and hidden in Me. This is why the fear is so compelling. It is real. Nevertheless, My bond-servants will, indeed, follow Me wherever I go at all cost to their own lives."

"Why is it so hard to leave Babylon? Why can't Christian people just walk away from it?"

"The spirits of Babylon are numerous and very compelling. At the head of the system is the mother of harlots, Jezebel. She is disguised as the bride and, thereby, has deceived the best of hearts. Yet, she is an enticing spirit. Her seductive ways appeal to the flesh of men and their desire for power, position, and riches. Working under her are all the Ahabs: the kings and rulers in the *churches*, spirits operating through prideful men. The Ahabs are the Nicolaitans—the conquerors of the people. They are the clergy system that elevates itself above the people. Working for them are such other demons as pride, haughtiness, control, position, authority, power, possessiveness, domination, ownership, jealousy.

"These spirits rule the *churches*, the systems, and the people under them. They rule through spirits of fear and intimidation. Co-operating with these are spirits of tradition, dogmatism, sectarian-ism, doctrine, sentimentalism, denominationalism; the warring spirits are confusion, hatred, division, divisiveness, bitterness, and the like. These have holds on men and are strongholds in the minds of men. But at the root of them all are the despicable spirits of religion.

"For men to come out, they must first understand these things. Then they must repent of them and come unto Me with a pure heart. I will deliver them. I will separate them and cleanse their defiled hearts. I will dress them in readiness and prepare them for My banqueting table. I will feed them the good fodder of My word in-stead of the indigestible twigs of men's mind. Who can digest the human intellect? Who can swallow its lies and deceits? The answer is everyone. For man is stupid and devoid of knowledge. But he who has My Spirit will hunger and thirst after Me, and I will reveal My nature to him. He will come unto Me, and I will sup with him and he with Me. He is the one who can come out of the harlot.

"He is the one who will come out of the harlot, for I shall lose not one whom the Father has given to Me—none, except the son of perdition.

"The harlot is everywhere. She is in the ministry, seeking to promote herself in power, position, and riches. She is in the minis-ters—the Ahabs, the Nicolaitans. She plays politics to promote her-self. She lies, cheats, defrauds; she will do anything to get ahead. She is full of ambition and selfish desires. She is an abomination to Me, the very opposite of My nature and of the nature of My bride.

"This, My son, is why I say a woman is to be quiet and gentle and submissive, for she bears the joy of the bride in her heart. She loves her lover. The harlot loves herself. The bride gives of herself. The harlot takes unto herself. The bride hides herself in hidden-ness. The harlot exposes herself—even in her doorway. She adver-tises herself and entices men to come into her, be joined to her for the pleasures of the flesh. Self is flesh. Anything for Self is flesh. This is why it is the abomination that makes desolate My holy place. My holy place is the spirit of men. When that spirit is defiled by the flesh, that is an abomination to Me.

"The harlot is the flesh nature of man that has taken its rule in the *churches*—self-aggrandizement, men seeking to increase them-selves in flocks. They count numbers and glory in them. They own their own sheep and call them Mine. They lie, for they are not My sheep. They make disciples unto themselves, of themselves, and for themselves. They fleece their flocks for their own sordid gain. These are not My ministers. They are hirelings and Nicolaitans.

"The harlot is ugly and hides her ugliness in gaudy garments and decorates her face in lavishing colors. She hides behind these things. She is ashamed of her sin. Yet, she will not repent. She cannot repent. She is evil from within."

"What about the harlot, Lord? Who or what is the harlot spirit? How can we know when she is operating?"

"The harlot spirit, My son, is anything for Self. She is the abomination that makes desolate My holy place. My bride, My holy bride is robed in righteousness. She has eyes only for Me. She is given wholly to Me. She is pure and undefiled and seeks nothing for herself. She is the laid-down life. She denies herself of Self, takes up her cross, and follows Me daily. My bride is beautiful and shines in the innocence of her holiness. She is separated unto Me. She is joined to Me. I am her husband and she is My only true love. I have birthed her. I have given her sup. I have adorned her in righteousness, beauty, and holiness. My bride is hard to see in the world because she is quiet, unassuming, gentle, meek—she is hidden in Me.

"But the harlot—she is loud and boisterous. She seeks herself. She wishes to expand her own bosom with the wealth of the nations. She seeks Self in everything, and everything she does is for Self. She has painted her face with all manner of atrocities. She loathes the bride. For she has no husband. She is a harlot. She takes anyone or anything into her bosom if it brings about an increase to her. She is an abomination to Me because she is full of boasting. She is deceitful. She is carnal. She is a harlot. A harlot is untrue. She is the counterfeit.

"Men come to her seeking Self—self-aggrandizement, self-reliance, self-pity, self-strength, self-anything. Self, Self, Self. This, My son, is how you can know if the harlot is at work: Ask yourself, 'Is what I am about to do, or is what I am discerning have to do with Self? Am I seeking Self? Or am I seeking the good of others?' If it is Self, it is the harlot every time. If it is from Me," says the Lord, "it will be for others; it will be the laid-down life of *agape.*

"She is a deceiver. She holds out all sorts of promises. She promises life and joy and prosperity and peace; and, in return, she charges a price. She cannot offer these things; for, in fact, those who go into her go down into Sheol—they go down into death, into poverty, into despair, into bondage and anguish.

"Ah, she cannot offer these things. Only I can offer life and joy and peace and blessing and happiness. These are found in Me. She says, take unto yourself what is yours. I say, lay it down. She says to live, drink, and be merry. I say, weep and mourn. She says, I will give you pleasure and great delight. But I say, I will give you life everlasting. Ah, she cannot offer you peace. She cannot offer you these things. They are not hers. She entices her lovers into thinking she holds these things, but she does not.

"The harlot is Self—anything for Self. You play the harlot when your heart goes after any substitute for Jesus.

"Remember this, My son, and guard your heart. Empty yourself of Self. Stay humble, broken, empty before Me. I will fill you up. I will be your joy, your satisfaction, your everything.

"Beware of the harlot. She is everywhere—in every window, every door, every street corner. She is in the voice of everyone who speaks. She is boasting, bragging, enticing, flattering, and seductive. Beware! Beware!

"The harlot is in the bosom of every man. She rises up and says I want this or that, or I want to do this or that, or I want to be this or that. At all times and in every way she seeks herself. Can you see her in the *church*? Can you see her in the ministry? Can you see her on the boards and committees, in places of high leadership? Can you see her in the pew? Can you see her in the choir? Everywhere she lifts her skirt to dance her own dance to the tune she has written in her own invention. And when she has finished, she takes her bows and receives her accolades, her applause, her plaques and trophies; she decks her walls with them. She is the harlot, the counterfeit to My bride who is simply hidden in Me."

"For whosoever will save his life shall lose it; but whosoever shall lose his life for My sake and the gospel's, the same shall save it." Mark 8:35.

* * *

The trumpet call is sounding:
"Come out of her, My people!"
"Let us go out to Him outside the camp, bearing His reproach." Heb. 13:13.

Dare we face our idols,
cleanse the temple, and
return to the God of our salvation?

Other books by the author:

The Crucified Ones intends to call forth a people to walk in radical obedience in preparation for the Lord's coming.

In Search of Dad is a book that intends to call forth that supernatural, transcending power that flows from Father-God, enabling men to be godly fathers to their families.

His Presence in the Midst of You is a book that intends to call forth a sanctified people to carry the ark of the Lord's Presence into the world around them.

These books are available without charge through Ingathering Press as God enables. The address for Ingathering Press is on the copyright page.

I pray for all who read these books that God may give you a spirit of wisdom and revelation in the knowledge of Him; that the eyes of your heart may be enlightened; that you may know the hope of His calling, what are the riches of the glory of His inheritance in the saints, and what is the surpassing greatness of His power toward you as a believer.